DISASTERS

eBooks / eChapters / Articles
eBooks
Browse Subject
Browse, Search, Read & Buy...
Subject Catalogues
eChapters
Publishers
Print Books
Forthcoming
eBooks
New Titles
scan for catalogue
NIPA
GENX
ONLINE RESOURCES
Publishing Books and Journals
Ebooks and e articles, Current Affairs
Reasoning, Logic and Aptitude
Competitive Examination Preparation
Language Learning and Development Programme
Document Quality Checker and Improvement Tool
Effective Public Speaking, Presentation and Interpersonal Skills
Online Programmes for Professional Development
Personality Development and Human Values
PAY USING
UPI
PayPal

DISASTERS

Strengthening Community Mitigation & Preparedness

Brig (Dr) B.K. Khanna

Senior Specialist (Training & Capacity Development)
National Disaster Management Authority
(An Apex Body of Government of India on Disaster Management)
Government of India, New Delhi

Nina Khanna

Senior Teacher
Convent of Jesus & Mary
New Delhi

New India Publishing Agency
Pitam Pura, New Delhi-110 088

Published by
Sumit Pal Jain *for*
New India Publishing Agency
101, Vikas Surya Plaza, CU Block, L.S.C. Mkt.,
Pitam Pura, New Delhi- 110 088, (India)
Phone: 011-27341717, Fax: 011-27341616
Mobile : 09717133558
E-mail: newindiapublishingagency@gmail.com
Web: www.bookfactoryindia.com

ISBN : 978-93-80235-45-5

Composed and Designed by NIPA

Dedicated

to the victims of

Disasters

Vice Chairman
National Disaster Management Authority
Government of India

FOREWORD

1. Indian Sub-continent is one of the most disaster prone areas of the World. India took a defining step by unanimously enacting Disaster Management (DM) Act 2005, institutionalizing DM framework in India at Centre, State, District and Local levels. National Disaster Management Authority (NDMA) was constituted, with the Prime Minister as its *ex-officio* Chairperson. Similar arrangements were also made at the State and District levels. Under the provisions of the DM Act, NDMA has formulated a National Policy on Disaster Management duly approved by the Government of India and disseminated to all concerned. In addition, NDMA has released guidelines on all specific types of natural disasters and related thematic issues. Guidelines have also been issued on man-made disasters.

2. Community is invariably taken as the first responder to any disaster. Recognizing its pre-eminence, the National Policy and Guidelines lay emphasis on the Community empowerment and preparedness. A well prepared and resilient community is better prepared to face the challenges of disasters and facilitates timely recovery. Of late, a large number of publications have come up on various facets of disaster management, yet a few authors have touched the core issue of strengthening community mitigation and preparedness. It is extremely heartening to see that this topic has been taken up by Brig Bhagat Khanna and Nina Khanna.

3. Brig Khanna has been with the NDMA for the last five years as a Senior Specialist, Training and Capacity Development. His practical experience in conduct of the mock exercises all over the Country has been amply exhibited in the thought process in this book. This is one of the most readable and practical exposition on the disaster management.

4. In fact, I have known Brig Khanna for the last over 33 years. Right from his Army days he has been writing on varied subjects. His first book, ***'All You Wanted to Know About Disasters',*** is again a very handy and a must read for all those who want to pursue disaster management as an academic discipline. Writing on disasters requires a blend of sensitivity, creativity and commitment which both Co-authors have amply exhibited.

5. I would like to compliment Bhagat and Nina Khanna for coming out with a topical book for the Community, on disasters in India. Conduct of mock exercises has been one of the most successful initiatives of the NDMA, which has been handled by Brig Khanna. The Chapter on conduct of mock exercises will greatly help the district administration, most accident hazard industries and the educational institutions in their preparedness to manage disasters effectively.

General NC Vij
PVSM, UYSM, AVSM (Retd.)

New Delhi
13 July, 2010

Dr. S.P. Agarwal
M.S. (Surg.) M.Ch. (Neuro.),
FIMSA, FICS, D.Sc (hon.)
(Former Director General Health
Services, Govt. of India)
Secretary General

Indian Red Cross Society
National Headquarters
1, Red Cross Road, New Delhi-110 001 (INDIA)
Tel. : 011-23716424, 23717063
Fax : 011-23717454
E-mail : spagarwalsg@indianredcross.org
spasgircs@gmail.com

MESSAGE

India has been managing disasters since time immemorial. The disasters were considered God's gift or wrath and hence the emphasis to manage them was relief centric. A string of major disasters in the last decade of 20th century and first decade of 21st century and international obligations, made the decision makers alter the approach to a holistic one, with emphasis on mitigation and preparedness. DM Act institutionalized this paradigm shift.

Indian Red Cross Society and St John Ambulance Brigade have been involved in mitigation, training and relief phases of disasters from their very inception. They have done a commendable job in the field of Disaster Management, with over 700 branches at District/sub district level in all the 35 States/UTs of the Indian Union, making it the largest humanitarian Organization in the country.

One of major initiative taken by the Society has been the starting of part time Post Graduate Diploma Course in 2006 on,' Disaster Preparedness & Rehabilitation', affiliated with GGS Indraprastha University, Delhi. Brig Khanna has been one of our distinguished faculty members. I have listened to most of his sessions and found them to be interesting, educative and informative, explained with practical experience.

The author's earlier book, 'All You Wanted to Know about Disasters', was received very well by the students and the faculty alike. The present book, 'Disasters : Strengthening Community Mitigation and Preparedness', is a comprehensive document on Disaster Management and deals with 11 perceived disasters, besides explaining on how to conduct mock exercises at the community/organization/industry/district level. It is a good reference book for the students and for faculty members. The Organizations and industries which have stake in disaster management will be able to derive maximum benefit from its contents.

New Delhi
13 July, 2010

Dr. S.P. Agarwal

PREFACE

This is my second book on spreading general awareness on disasters especially at individual, family and community levels. The response to the first book on, 'All you wanted to know about disasters' encouraged me to share my knowledge and experience acquired over the last five years serving NDMA with the readers. My better-half, who has also since acquired MBA degree in Disaster Management helped me in all the field and analytical work and graciously joined me as my co-author. Since my last book, I joined the National Disaster Management Authority on 09 August 2005, much before its constitution, on 28 Sep. 2005, at the behest of Gen NC Vij, its founding Vice Chairman. Hence I can proudly say that I was part of the support team which raised this apex body on DM in India. This gave me an opportunity to be involved in formulation of national policy on DM, issuance of guidelines on various types of disasters and other initiatives taken by it. The Vice Chairman, specifically entrusted me with the task of implementation of the initiative of inculcating the culture of preparedness in the community and the first responders in the country. This was to be executed through conduct of table top & mock exercises on various types of perceived disasters. Starting from scratch, this initiative has taken off in the right direction and has aroused enthusiastic and overwhelming response from community, first responders, district administration and state authorities. Post Mumbai 26/11 terrorist attacks, even the private organizations have been approaching for help in putting their DM plans in place and getting them validated through mock exercises. For this singular achievement I can take some credit as I gave the indigenous initiative a practical shape. The interaction with community, district/tehsil/taluk/sub-division level functionaries, the DM planners in the state, NGOs, schools/educational institutions, National Disaster Response Force, Para Military Forces, Armed Forces and most accident hazardous industries, enriched my knowledge about management of disasters. So far (July 2010) NDMA has conducted over 215 mock exercises in 35 states/UTs, 91 districts, 49 MAH industrial units and 99 schools. These mock exercises were conducted on perceived hazards, like earthquakes, floods, urban flooding, cyclones, urban fires, chemical (industrial) disasters, terrorist related disasters, mass casualty management, *etc*. Some of the lessons learnt from these mock exercises have been included in this book. As we go to Press, I have also been detailed to help in preparing the stake-holders of Commonwealth Games, New Delhi 2010, to manage all types of natural and manmade disasters.

I am indebted to Gen VC Vij, Vice Chairman, NDMA for giving me opportunity to broaden my knowledge on disaster management. I am thankful to the founding members of NDMA, namely Lt Gen (Dr) JR Bhardwaj, Sh Mohan Kanda, Sh M Shashidhar Reddy, Prof NVC Menon, Sh KM Singh, Sh JK Sinha, Mrs PJ Rao and Sh B Bhattacharjee, for their advice and encouragement in the performance of my duties. My sincere gratitude to Mr.Nirankar Saxena (Director- FICCI), Major General R.K. Kaushal and Nawal Prakash for their continued support. I am thankful to Dr SP Agarwal, Secretary General, Indian Red Cross Society and Prof Amarjeet Kaur, Dean, Centre for Disaster Management Studies, GGS Indraprastha University, Delhi for giving me opportunity to interact with their PG and MBA students, respectively.

I will be failing in my duty on personal level if I did not thank my sons Deepak and Amith and daughters-in-law Namrita and Yeshey, my most darling grandson Aaryan and most loved grand daughter Yeshami, for their continued love and moral support. I am also grateful to the entire Staff of New India Publishing Agency, for their faith in me, especially Sumit Pal Jain.

July, 2010

Brig (Dr) B.K. Khanna
Nina Khanna

CONTENTS

❑❑❑

Chapter 1

Introduction

The aim of this book is to further strengthen the knowledge of readers on management of disasters so that they are better prepared to cope with more frequently occurring natural and manmade disasters.

The process that helps us to face disasters effectively is commonly known as disaster preparedness. When a disaster strikes, it affects us directly and immediately. While as the government, international agencies such as United Nations, Red Cross Society, non government organizations, like Ramakrishna Mission, OXFAM, CARE, resident welfare associations in urban areas and panchayats in rural areas assist us when faced with disasters the community, invariably remains the first responders. Hence, the individuals as a part of community should prepare adequately to prevent, face and respond to disasters effectively. History has shown that where communities have prepared adequately to confront disasters, losses to life and property have been less and environment could be protected. People living in an area may be prone to more than one type of disaster. For example Kutch District of Gujarat is vulnerable to floods, drought, cyclones and to earthquakes. Such an area is called 'multiple hazard' zone. The country is divided into various hazard zones depending upon the vulnerability of the area to various disasters. When these zones overlap, we have an overlap hazard zone. That leads us to the question, what is a hazard?

What is a Hazard?

Hazard is a dangerous natural or man made condition or event, that has the potential of causing injury, loss of life or damage to property, livelihood or/and environment. A hazard could be natural hazard, like earthquake, cyclone, tsunami, flood, drought, forest fire, sea crosion *etc.* Man made hazards include explosions, leakage of toxic gases, pollution, dam failures, urban fires, urban flooding, mine disasters, ship wreck and accidents, like rail, road, boat and air. Wars, insurgencies, civil strife, riots and terrorist related activities, like the Mumbai attacks 26/11, are included in human indeaced disasters.

What is Vulnerability?

Vulnerability is the extent to which a community, structure, service or geographic area is likely to be damaged or disrupted by the impact of a particular hazard. It could be due to several causes present in the community itself, like poverty, lack of information, poor living conditions, overloading poorly maintained equipment, inadequate safety precautions, bad construction and proximity to hazardous terrain or a disaster prone area. Vulnerability precedes disasters, contribute to their severity, impede disaster response and may continue to exist long after a disaster has struck. It is vulnerability and hazard that turn the situation into a risk or possibility of a disaster in an area. Vulnerability broadly can be divided into physical or socio-economic vulnerability.

What is Risk?

Risk is a measure of the potential to cause damage. High vulnerability and high hazard are associated with high disaster risk. If either vulnerability or hazard is low, disaster risk would be less. Disaster risk can be called the product of hazard and vulnerability divided by the capacity. Capacity could be defined as the capability of the community to intervene and manage a hazard in order to reduce its potential impact. Conventionally risk is expressed by the equation.

$$\text{Risk} = \frac{\text{Hazard} \times \text{Vulnerability}}{\text{Capacity}}$$

What is Disaster or Calamity?

A disaster refers to a catastrophe, mishap, calamity or grave occurrence from natural or manmade causes which is beyond the coping capacity of the affected community. Disaster results in widespread human fatalties and is accompanied by loss of livelihood and/or property, assets, public infrastructure and environment. Hazards cannot be prevented but their effects can be minimised by taking precautionary measures and from becoming disasters.

- A disaster disrupts normal functioning of society. It affects large number of people.
- It causes large scale loss of life and property.
- It affects a community which requires external aid to cope with the losses.
- Effect of disaster can be minimised by taking precautionary measures.

Disaster Management Cycle

There are three key stages of activities in disaster management:

- *Before a Disaster (Pre Disaster):* to develop the capacity and create resilience in the community and responders to minimise human, material or environmental losses caused by hazards.
- *During a Disaster:* to ensure that the needs and provisions of victims are met to alleviate their sufferings.
- *After a Disaster (Post Disaster):* to achieve rapid and durable recovery which does not reproduce the original vulnerable conditions. The aim should be to build back better.

The general belief is that disaster management refers to only in terms of the emergency rescue and relief period and post disaster rehabilitation. This is due to these two components being strong in terms of high profile visibility, political support and funding provisions. While response, relief and rehabilitation are important and vital activities, successful disaster management planning must encompass the complete realm of activities and situations that occur before, during and after a disaster. These phases are represented as a cycle or continuum, which, if circumstances allow reduce the negative effects of future disasters. The different phases of disaster management can best be visualised as a disaster management cycle as explained in the diagram (Fig. 1.1)

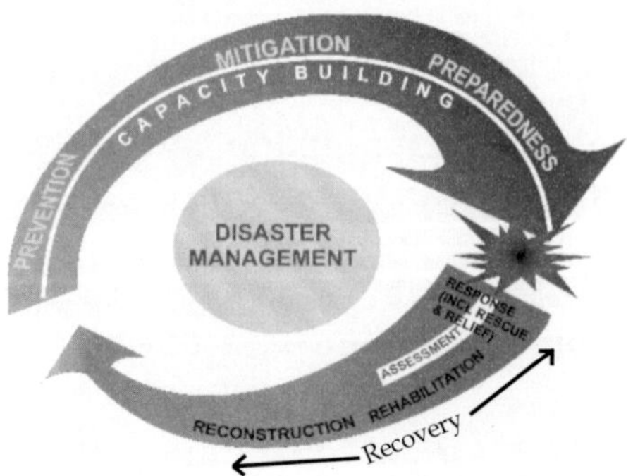

Fig. 1.1 Disaster Management Cycle

Important activities in each phase of the cycle are as follows:

a) Prevention and Mitigation

- Preventing construction of vital infrastructures and habitation in risk zones.
- Land use planning.
- Making laws, manuals, standard operating procedures and checklists.
- Disaster resistant buildings as per National Building Code.
- Encouragement to community to construct build/retrofit buildings which are disaster resistant by giving them incentives, like income tax rebate.
- Community awareness and education through information, education and communication (IEC) material.
- Retrofitting weak buildings.
- Risk transfer through micro finance and micro insurance.
- Capacity building of community and first responders.
- Preparation of disaster management plans for families, community/schools/colleges, malls, cinema houses and each building.

b) Preparedness

- Raising, equipping and training of National Disaster Response Force/State Disaster Response Force.

- Mock drills, table top and simulation exercises.
- Making inventory of resources, both trained manpower and material.
- Establish, upgrade and modernise forecasting and early warning systems.
- Real time dissemination of warnings and information to local authorities and community.
- Identifying vulnerable groups and managing their requirements.
- Building capacity for immediate and effective response at local, district, state and national level. Stream line responses of all stake holders.

c) Response, Assessment and Immediate Relief

- Activate emergency operation centre (EOC) at district level. Incident commander is nominated and all emergency support functionarics report at EOC. Incident Command Posts at sub-division/taluk/tehsil level, if disaster is big.
- Implement Disaster Management Plans. Start issuing periodic situation reports.
- Deploy self contained search and rescue teams (local, state, NDRF) as per requirement.
- Nominated medical response teams get activated. First priority to evacuate and attending injured. Evacuation of injured after TRIAGE and Stablizing condition of victims through first aid.
- Setting up of temporary relief camps and evacuate affected people. Start community kitchens with help of Non Government/ Voluntary/Government Organisations. Ensure proper drinking water and Sanitation.
- Cater for requirement of cattles and animals.

- Mobilizing other required resources.
- Make immediate assessment of damages and requirements.
- Disposal of dead – human and animals caracasses.
- Management of NGOs for optimum utilization of their potential.
- Management of media (print and electronic).

d) Recovery and Rehabilitation
- Removal of debris.
- Making community aware on the health and safety measures.
- Restoration of sanitation
- Restoring essential services like water, electricity and communication links.
- Providing temporary interim dwellings
- Providing relief interim – financial and in lieu as per Relief Manual.
- Restoring employment opportunities.
- Counseling trauma cases.
- Reconstruction of new houses and repairing damaged ones. Owner driven reconstruction preferred. Every disaster to be considered as opportunity to build back better.

Disaster Risk Management

Disaster risk management has three components:

i. Risk identification and assessment.

ii. Risk reduction.

iii. Risk transfer.

Disaster Risk Identification and Assessment would help the community to assess the hazards in which they are living like earthquakes, floods, cyclones, urban fires, terrorist related acivities *etc* which threaten the community and enhance its vulnerabilities. The assessment evaluates the elements which are at risk and analyses the causes of vulnerable conditions. This includes physical, geographical, social, political and psychological factors that cause certain category of people to be more vulnerable to various hazards than others.

Disaster Risk Reduction: It includes all measures, which reduce disaster related loss of life, property or assets by either reducing the hazard or vulnerability. An element is said to be at risk when it is exposed to hazards and is likely to be affected by the impact of those hazards. Risk reduction has three components *viz.* Preparedness, Mitigation and Prevention.

Preparedness

Preparedness is at local, district, state and national level. At local level it is the responsibility of the community and local self government. They manage it through locally constituted Disaster Management Committees and/or teams. At district level, disaster management plans are made and the Collector/Deputy Commissioner is responsible for preparing, implementing and monitoring them. District Disaster Management Authority (DDMA) as per DM Act 2005 is headed by the Collector and is co-chaired by local elected representative. DDMA is constituted by the State Govt. and members from departments like police, medical, fire services, civil defence municipal corporation etc. At State level, it is Secretary, Disaster Management (erstwhile relief commissioner) who is responsible to prepare the State Disaster Management Plan. State Level Disaster Management Authority is headed by the Chief Minister with Chief Secretary as Member Secretary. He also heads State Executive Committee. At national level, the National Disaster Management Authority is headed by the Prime Minister, with a Vice Chairman and eight Members. It is mandated to formulate national DM policy and approves National DM Plan. It also issues guidelines on various types of disasters.

Mitigation

Mitigation involves structural and non-structural measures undertaken to limit the adverse impact of natural hazards, environmental degradation and technological hazards.

Structural Mitigation

- *Engineered Structures:* These are structures which are designed and constructed by qualified architects, engineers and masons. Disaster resistant construction is achieved by :

- Assessing the vulnerability of the area against natural and manmade disasters.
- Planning structural measures to resist the effect of such vulnerabilities.
- Locating buildings in a safe place.
- Construction with suitable material in right mix.
- Construction under trained masons, engineers and architects.
- Construction as per national building bye laws/codes.
- Retroffiting buildings/structures if required to make them disaster resistant.

❐ *Non Engineered Structures:* These are constructions built by owners through masons turned contractors. There is a need to train masons even for constructing traditionally designed non engineered structures.

Non Structured Mitigation

❐ *Legal Framework*: Revising State Disaster Management laws in consonance with DM Act 2005 and national guidelines on Earthquakes, to prevent illegal constructions and take legal action against defaulters. Revision of municipal regulations and sound compliance regime with binding consequences.

❐ *Land Use Planning:* Control of human activities including infrastructures in the hazard prone areas, to avoid loss of human lives and property.

❐ *Incentives and Financial Framework:* Government grants or subsidies for people who undertake mitigation measures in their buildings/structures. Insurance companies can offer discounts on premiums for home loans. Banks can offer easy loans for retrofitting and constructing new disaster resistant buildings. Government can also give tax exemption for expenditure on constructing disaster resistant houses/structures or retrofitting them.

❐ *Training and Education:* Providing awareness and know how to Government officials involved in management of disasters, in construction (engineers, architects, masons *etc.*), craftsmen, land use planners and the community encouraging them to adopt mitigation.

- *Public Awareness*
  - A good public knowledge and understanding of hazards and vulnerabilities.
  - Awareness campaign through print and electronic media.
  - Effective mitigation and monitoring measures.
  - Public participation in community preparedness programs.
  - Community participation during mock drills on various types of disasters, organised at local, district, state and NDMA level.

Prevention

Prevention is all actions taken to prevent a hazard from becoming disaster, including making preventive laws and monitoring mechanism. Although all kinds of disasters need to be prevented, prevention, perse is more applicable to manmade and technological disasters. Stringent safety precautions through technological innovations can bring changes. Natural hazards cannot be prevented but if the vulnerability of community is reduced, one can prevent a hazard from becoming a disaster. Proper socio-economic development and active continum ownership, participation of communities in disaster management and development of adequate warning system, where applicable, can bring positive results. Critical infrastructures like dams, bridges etc. need to be constantly monitored for safety standards.

Risk Transfer

Risk transfer is tool to ensure that losses from disasters are compensated or recovered by individuals or community. Examples are insurance of home, crops, equipment *etc*. Community contingency funds are created through disaster management planning that put aside certain amount of money contributed by community for use in emergencies. In developed countries, private insurance sector is a major contributor for funding reconstruction after a disaster. In developing countries Government and individuals take up major burden of cost of disaster related losses.

Levels of Disasters

For convenience of their management, disasters are classified in four levels.

- *Level 'O':* All activities before a disaster strikes comes under 'O' Level. It includes formulation of disaster management plan, capacity building, construction of disaster resistant buildings especially lifeline buildings, retrofitting weak buildings, training of architects, engineers, masons, artisans *etc.;* mock drills to validate plans and updating, identification of available resources and networking, between community, village panchayat, taluk, tehsil, resident welfare association, district level training of all stake holders, identifying the vulnerable groups and catering for their safety, legal framework, spreading general awareness, *etc.*
- *Level 1:* Disasters which can be managed within the resources available at district level. Examples are road accidents, boat capsizing and low level riots. Domestic fires also come under this level.
- *Level 2:* Disasters which can be managed at the state level, under overall guidance of State Disaster Management Authority. The coordination is done by Secretary, Disaster Management through state emergency operation centre. The activation of resources take place on orders of heads of Emergency Support Functionary (ESF). There may be movement of personnel and material from one district to another within the State. Examples are low intensity cyclones, floods and even mild intensity earthquakes. In manmade disasters, rail accidents, multiple road accidents, urban fires, forest fires *etc* fall under Level 2 disasters.
- *Level 3:* All disasters which are outside the coping capacity of the State and require intervention from the Central Government come under Level 3 disasters. Coordination between States and International help is managed by NDMA on behalf of Central Government. Bhuj earthquake, Tsunami 2004 and Orissa Super Cyclone 1999, come under Level 3 disasters. Entry points (air, road and rail) are designated for receiving relief material, accounting for and distribution as per demand.

- States are basically responsible to manage disaster in their own states.
- Central Government plays the role of facililator for co-ordination support in terms of manpower, material and financial assistance.

Chapter 2

Types of Disasters

The United Nations had declared the decade of 90s (1990-1999) as the International Decade for National Disaster Risk Reduction to enable developing countries to build up their capacity to cope up with disasters. The Government of India also set up a High Powered Committee (HPC), in August 1999, to review the preparedness and mitigation of natural and manmade disasters and recommend measures for strengthening the organisational structures and a comprehensive model plan for management of disasters at national, state and district level. The HPC after due deliberatons submitted the report in Feb. 2001. The HPC identified the disasters under the following types (categories) :

I - Water & Climate related disasters

II - Geologically related disasters

III - Chemical, industrial & nuclear related disasters

IV - Accident related disasters

V - Biologically related disasters

I have added one more group i.e. terrorist related disasters

Type I - Water and Climate Related Disasters

These include a wide variety of meteorological, hydrological and climate phenomena that pose a threat to life, property and the environment. The hydro-meteorological hazards include :

1. Flood and Drainage Management
2. Drought
3. Cyclones
4. Tornadoes and Hurricanes
5. Hailstorm
6. Cloudburst
7. Snow Avalanche
8. Heat and Cold Waves
9. Sea Erosion
10. Thunder and lightning

The spatial and temporal scales of these hazards vary widely from short lived, violent phenomena of limited extent to large systems. These events can subject large regions to disastrous weather phenomena, like strong winds, heavy flood-producing rains, heavy snow-fall, blizzard conditions, freezing rains and extreme hot or cold temperature conditions for periods of several days. The application of meteorological, climatological and hydrological knowledge in the area of disaster management has a very significant role to play in the assessment of risk, land-use planning and the designing of structures which greatly contribute to disaster mitigation. The classical forcasting and warning role, the provision of warnings of impending severe weather, extreme temperatures, drought or floods, contribute to preparedness. Updated warnings, forecasts, observations and consultations with emergency and relief agencies contribute to the response phase. Finally, special forecasts and other advice assist recovery operations. Floods, extreme temperatures, high winds and droughts may cause or exacerbate other disasters. These include possible risks of wild fires, insect and pest infection, toxic gas releases, oil spills and nuclear accidents. Therefore, the provision of meteorological advice and products such as trajectory forecasts or advise based on dispersal modelling can represent a valuable contribution to addressing other non-hydrometerological hazards.

Type II - Geological Disasters

Geological disasters would include

1. Earthquakes
2. Landslides and Mudflows
3. Dam failure / Dam bursts
4. Mine fires

68.7% of the country lies in high to moderate seismic zones that could have damaging seismic intensity. 3% of Indian landmass is affected by landslides, which are wide spread in the Himalayas (covering J&K, Himachal, Uttarakhand and NE States) and the Western Ghats. Comprehensive guidelines on management of earthquakes were issued by NDMA in May 2007, which are available on its site <*www.ndma.gov.in*>. Earthquakes are being monitored by India Meteorological Department, Survey of India, National Geophysical Research Institute, I.I.T. Roorkee and I.I.T. Mumbai. Maps have been prepared which help in classifying the country, into earthquake hazard zones. The vulnerability atlas gives state and district wise hazards to buildings and other infrastructure due to natural disasters. The disaster can be made much worse due to the vulnerability of the community itself. Emergency measures of evacuation, search, rescue and relief form important action plans in disaster management. Once disaster occurs, disaster management machinery should plunge into action in rescue and relief operections as per trigger mechanism preparedness plan. Rapid damage assessment for emergency relief, documentation of damages and losses and reconstruction with strategy to build back better are important aspects of managing disasters.

Landslides and mudflows are predictable and the damage minimized or even averted with proper and systematic studies and with adoption of remedial measures. Measures for landslide control are avoidance, surface drainage, sub-surface drainage, supporters, excavation, river structural work, vegetation, blasting and hardening. Dambursts/Dam failure releases large quantities of water causing disastrous damage to down stream installations, disrupting socio-economic activities causing loss of life with adverse ecological and environmental impacts. The structural stability of a dam can be threatened by floods, rockslides, landslides, earthquakes, deterioration of the heterogeneous foundation, poor quality of construction, differential settlement, improper management and acts of war. The three types of earth embankment problems commonly found are seepage, slope stability and vegetation outgrowth. Extreme floods and uncertain geologic setting are the principal causes of dam breaches. Further, the earth fill dams have been involved in largest number of failures, followed by gravity dams, rock fills and multiple and single arches. Disaster mitigation encompass a wide range of options, ranging from issuance of flood warnings to reduction of flooding to active evacuation. The effectiveness of these programs depend upon accuracy of flood forecasting and management and cooperation between public and respective management agency.

Mini fires are caused due to spontaneous heating of coal and carbonaceous matter in the rocks. In coal mines the fires could be underground fires which have remained underground or may become surface fires, fires is coal benches in open cast mines, fires in overlying rock mass, fires in overburden dumps or fires in coal stacks. Combacting mine fires, specially underground fires that have remained underground or those that have become surface fires is a costly proposition. The trigger mechanism should aim at preventing any further occurrence of the fires and quick liquidation of existing fires. During preparedness, zoning of existing coal mine fire affeted regions, modelling/simulation of potential land subsidence and related impact, assessment of loss of property/energy; real time monitoring of coal fires for warning/prediction, pollution extent, ways to arrest fire, supporting affected population, awareness generation, relocation of affected people, should be visualised, analysed and finalized as response plan. Directorate General of Mine Safety examines all aspects of management of mines.

Type III - Chemical/Industrial/Nuclear Disasters

Disasters coming under this group includes :

1. Chemical/Industrial disasters
2. Nuclear Disasters

The chemical industrial disasters are in two categories viz 'on site' emergency and 'off site' emergency. 'On site' emergences include managing the disaster within the boundaries of the industrial unit and is operationalized by the industrial units own fire & emergency services, search & rescue and medical response teams. The evacuation within the unit premises is also ordered and carried out by the unit itself. When the emergency goes beyond the boundaries of the industrial unit and start affecting the nearby population and neighbouring industrial units, the district collector takes over as incident commender or nominate and incident commander an manage the disaster through the concept of incident response system. All the stakeholders viz police, fire services, medical services, civil defence, municipal corporation, PWD, supplies, electricity, water deptt, public relation officer, NGOs, volunters send their nodal officers at the incident command post which acts as control room and manages the disaster by optimizing resources. In nuclear disasters, the main vulnerability is during transportation, some accident taking place or nuclear leaks in the nuclear facilities. Managing the nuclear disasters within the nuclear facility is that of the unit itself. Atomic Energy Regulatory Board monitors all nuclear accidents and coordinates its management. Outside the nuclear facility, the district administration is responsible. Approximately 16 km around the nuclear facility, no habitation should come up. NDRF teams are capable of managing NBC disasters. Besides, BARC, Trombay and Army authorities have their response teams to react fast and support the efforts of NDRF.

Type IV - Accident Related Disasters

The dicasters which come under this group are :

1. Forest Fires
2. Urban Fires
3. Major Building Collapse
4. Mine Flooding
5. Oil Spill
6. Festival related disasters
7. Electrical disasters and fires
8. Air, road and rail accidents
9. Boat Capsizing
10. Village Fires
11. Ship Wreck

There is a need for vulnerability analysis of each individual type of hazard. Chances of survival of victims depend on quick response. Broadly, the actions would include informing the nearest police post/

station through mobile phone / land line or through passing vehicle, rescue those who are still trapped and can be easily rescued without aggravating their injuries, transportation of injured to nearest medical facility by first available means separating dead bodies to avoid obstructions for responders, traffic control using available manpower to avoid traffic jams, discourage people from crowding and prevent looting of goods. The basic responsibility for rescue, relief, evacuation, rehabitation measures, rebuilding of structures is that of the District Administration under District Collector. In case of accidents involving large caseulties, the police should first cordon the area and guard it, the fire & emergency services, civil defence and volunters should rescue the trapped people, the medical services should provide first aid at site, triage the patients for according priority and evacuate them in ambulances to the nearest/designated hospitals. The media should be managed well and not allowed to create panic, speculation or even distortion of facts. Media should be briefed at regular intervals and incident commander should address them as early as possible but atleast once in a day. Information centre should be established at incident command post (ICP) for answering queries from relatives/friends. A toll free number should also be set up at ICP at the earliest by BSNL/ MTNL. ICP will act as control room and coordinate the activities of all stakeholders.

Type V - Biological Disasters

The disasters in this category include :

1. Epidemics and biological disasters
2. Pest Attacks
3. Cattle Epidemics
4. Food Poisoning

Our response to these diseases were almost forgotten, till we had bird-flu and swing flu, which shook the world. The ash disaster over europe has also aroused fear of breathing related diseases. The biological disasters are rare but unless preparetions are made beforehand, they can have serious consequences. The disease burden due to communicable diseases in India is perhaps the highest in the World. Scarcity and poor water management across the country gives rise to various water borne infections and also provides suitable environment for vectors of a large number of diseases. Government is required to create infrastructure for emergency medical response. The high-tech laboratories have to be created with committed and trained professionals, enhancing the skills of the existing staff at various levels, early identification of such infections, investigation of out breaks and institution of specific control measures. NDMA has issued specific guidelines for, mass casuality management and hospital preparedness, 'biological disasters' and on Avian and swine flu specifics. These give out broad guidelines for the Ministry of Health and Family Welfare, who have to formulate action plan on it. State Government/UT Administration would include the directions in their State/UT disaster management plans.

Type VI - Terrorist Related Disasters

The disasters which can be included in this category are :

1. Serial Bomb Blast
2. Hostage Rescue
3. Hijacking
4. Riots
5. Terrorist storming/attack

These are highly sensitive and secretive disasters but get magnified due to their wide coverage and effect. At the centre level there is a National Crisis Management Committee headed by the Cabinet Secretary with secretarys of ministries, concerned with managing crisis, as Members. They are supposed to assemble immediately after a national level crisis and control and coordinate response. At the state level there is State Crisis Group headed by the Chief Secretary, with concerned secretarys of ministries/department as members. All state level emergencies are handled by this group. At individual level if you see any suspicious unattended item, report to Police/PCR, keep tenants after ascertaining their antecedents and sell your vehicle after due verification. But, if you get stuck in such an emergency (terrorist related), hit the ground, cover your head with arm and remain in that position till you can move to a safe place. Thereafter do not stay in the area, unless you can contribute to investigation. Never run when you are caught in a cross fire. In a bomb blast case also, taking position on ground immediately might save you from splinter injuries. If you are caught in a high jack, obey initially what the hijackers instruct. They are initially very jittery and trigger happy. One should not be foolhardy to take undesirable action with serious consequences. If however the hijackers are heading for delibrate crash into a national asset, efforts to over power them can be taken as that may be the only option left. "In a riot situation, move out of the area as early as possible. There an no pre-conceived solutions to such disasters. But basic precautionary measures should be taken to stay alive, to fight another disaster.

Analytical details of key disasters are given in subsequent chapters.

Chapter 3

Floods

Introduction

India is the most flood affected nation in the world after Bangladesh. It accounts for one fifth of global deaths due to floods and on an average 30 million people are affected every year. Unprecedented floods take place every year in one or the other state of the country.

Floods have been recurrent phenomenon in India since time immemorial. The annual average precipitation including snowfall over India is estimated at 1200 mm, 80% of which occurs in the monsoon season. Rainfall varies widely across the length and breadth of the country. The result is devastating; floods in some parts of the country and drought conditions in other parts. On an average 1500 human lives are lost and nearly one lac (1,00,000) livestock die annually, due to floods and drought.

Inadequate capacity of the rivers to contain within their banks and the high flows following heavy rainfall, lead to flooding. Area with poor-drainage characteristics get flooded by accumulation of rain water.

Hilly and not too hilly regions with heavy rainfall/thunderstorms/cloudbursts are prone to flash floods. Depressions, cyclonic storms, sudden release of water from the reservoirs, breaches in flood embankments, dams and cause landslide in dams and release of water due to melting of glacial icebergs lead to flash floods.

The river erosion is a result of the tendency of rivers to braid, meander and split with branches.

The problem of flooding and drainage congestion in urban areas is a recent phenomenon and is a result of encroachments in flood plains and waterways and lack of drainage network.

Rivers originating in China, Nepal and Bhutan cause severe floods in the states of Jammu & Kashmir, Himachal Pradesh, Uttar Pradesh, Bihar, West Bengal, Arunachal Pradesh and Assam.

Initiatives by the Government of India (GoI)

GoI has from time to time appointed Committees to look into the problem of floods and their management. Some of the important ones are: the Policy Statement of 1954, the Rashtriya Barh Ayog (1978) and the Task Force on Flood Management/Erosion Control (2004). However, the implementation of the recommendations has been rather slow.

Institutional Mechanism

As per the provisions of the Constitution of India, the primary responsibility for flood control lies with the States. At the centre level, Ministry of Home Affairs, the Ministry of Water Resources alongwith Central Water Commission, Brahmaputra Board, Ganga Flood Control Commission, India Meteorological Department and National Remote Sensing Agency look after various aspects of flood management. By the DM Act 2005, National Disaster Management Authority (NDMA) has been mandated with the responsibility of prevention, preparedness, mitigation, rehabilitation, reconstruction, recovery and formulation of appropriate policies and guidelines for management of various disasters. National Disaster Response Force (NDRF) provides specialized response to disasters.

At the State level, DM departments/Relief Commissioners, State Disaster Management Authority, headed by the Chief Minister, the District Disaster Management Authority headed by the District Magistrate, besides the Irrigation/Water Resources/Flood Control/Public Works departments deal with flood management. State Disaster Response Forces (SDRFs) are being raised out of State Armed Forces.

Out of the loans and grants by the Centre, allocations for the flood prone areas are made by state governments. There are also a few centrally sponsored/central sector schemes to assist them in this field. Under Calamity Relief Fund, provision is made for urgent relief and immediate repairs to the infrastructure damaged in floods. The National Flood Mitigation Project as proposed by NDMA forms part of the XI Plan to assist them in flood management.

This results in almost all rivers carrying heavy discharge during this period of four months. The flood hazard gets compounded by problems of sediment deposition, drainage congestion and synchronisation of river floods with sea tides in the coastal plains. Vulnerable area for floods is 46 million hectares, average area affected by floods annually is about 7.51 million hectares and area prone to water logging drainage congestion is a mha. Average yearly damage due to floods is about Rs. 1800 crore, effecting 32.03 million population.

Causes of Floods

Flood conditions may occur due to

- River in spate due to excessive rainfall in river catchments or concentration of runoff from the tributaries and rivers carrying flows in excess of their capacities.
- Snow melt
- Storm surges
- Short intense storms causing flash floods.

Flooding in rivers is mainly caused by

- Inadequate capacity within the banks of the river to contain high flows.
- River bank erosion and silting of riverbeds.
- Intense rainfall when river is flowing full.
- Landslides leading to obstruction of flow and change in the river course.
- Synchronisation of flood peaks in the main and tributary rivers.
- Flow retardation due to tidal and back water effects.
- Poor natural drainage systems.
- Cyclone and heavy rainfall when El Nino effect is on decline.

Characteristics of Floods

Floods may be measured and analysed by following criteria(s).

Depth of Water : Building foundations and vegetation will have different degrees of tolerance to bring inundated water.

Duration : Damage or degree of damage to structures, infrastructure and vegetation is often related to length of time with water inundation.

Velocity : Dangerously high velocities of flow may create erosive forces and hydrodynamic pressure which may destroy or weaken foundation supports. This may occur on the floodplains or in the main river channel.

Rate of Rise : Estimation of the rate of rise and discharge of a river is important as a basis for flood warning, evacuation plans and zoning regulations.

Frequency of Occurrence : The cumulative effect and frequency of occurrence measured over a long period of time will determine what type of construction or agricultural activities should take place on the flood plain.

Seasonality : Flooding during sowing or growing season may completely destroy the crop while cold weather floods from snowmelts may seriously affect the functioning of a community.

Flood Disaster Management

Flood Disaster Management can be classified into four major groups:

Attempts to modify the flood system, by taking physical measures such as:

- Construction of embankments.
- Construction of detention reservoirs.
- Channel improvement.

Attempts to modify the susceptibility to flood damage : It involves designed action to reduce the vulnerability of property and other developmental activities in the flood plains.

Attempts to modify the loss burden : It consists of uniformity in action to transform the incidence of losses, by spreading them over a large segment of community.

The loss bearing : Bearing the loss means 'Living with Floods'.

Flood Mitigation

Measures adopted for flood mitigation can be categorized into two groups, namely structural and non-structural.

Structural (Physical) Measures

Structural measures are physical in nature and aim to prevent flood waters from reaching potential damage centers. The important ones are flood embanements, dams, reservoirs, detention basins, channel improvement works, desilting / dredging of rivers, drainage improvement works, diversion of flood waters, catchment area treatment /afforestation measures, anti erosion works etc. Flood embankments, roads and railway lines are required to be aligned, located and designed properly and provisioned with adaquate water ways. The effectiveness of reservoirs in modrating floods can be optimized by having proper forecast of rainfall and inflows into the reservoirs, operating them according to laid down procedures.

The general approach of structural measures is to prevent flood water from reaching potential damage centers. The structural measures can be grouped into following:

- Dams and Reservoirs
- Embankments, flood walls, sea walls
- Natural detention basin
- Channel improvement
- Drainage improvement
- Diversion of flood waters

For effective functioning of physical measures, it is necessary that pre and post monsoon checks be made and special repairs carried out prior to flood period.

Non Structural Measures

Aim of non structural measures is to keep people away from floods. Various non structural measures are as follows:-

- Modifying the susceptibility to flood damages through flood plain management, flood proofing including disaster preparedness and response planning & flood forecasting & warning.
- Modifying the flood loss burden through disaster relief and flood fighting including public health measures.

Flood Mapping : Satellite data can be used very effectively for mapping and monitoring the flood inundated areas. It is useful for flood damage assessment, flood hazard zoning and post flood survey of river configuration and protection works.

Flood Proofing : Such measures help greatly in mitigation of disasters to the population in flood prone area. It is essentially a combination of structural change and emergency action without evacuation. A program of the flood proofing provides raised plat-forms as flood shelters for human beings and cattles, through raising the public utility installations above flood levels.

Flood Fighting : On receipt of flood forecasts, the flood forecasting stations (agencies) disseminate flood warnings to the officials concerned and the people of the affected area, to take necessary precautionary measures, like strengthening of the flood protection and mitigation works, evacuation of people to safer places, *etc.* The essential material is stocked in advance at appropriate places and measures for distribution of supplies are initiated to mitigate the miseries.

Flood Forecasting and Warning : It is given by Central Water Commission which has set up over flow flood monitoring and forecasting stations in different river-rain locations, covering major parts of the country. Accuracy of such forecast has been assessed between 93.4 to 97.5%. With acquisition of more modern gadgets, the efforts are to increase the forcast accuracy.

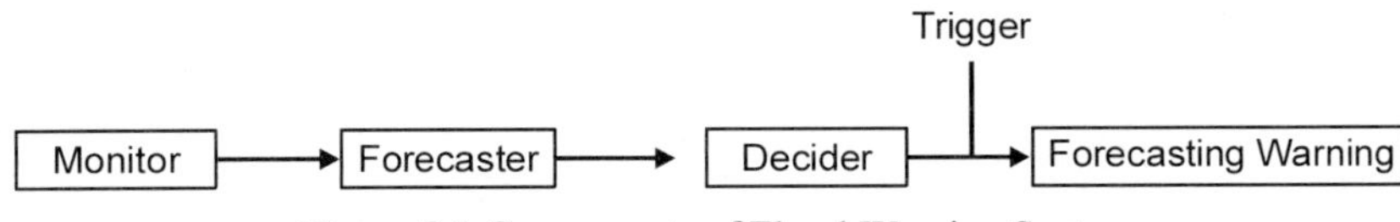

Figure 3.1 Components of Flood Warning System

Flood Insurance : Flood Insurance System is prevalent in developed country but in developing countries it is not given priority. In India, it has been initiated recently. It has several advantages and means to modify the burden of loss. It is being provided to cover the flood risk on a limited and selective scale. This is mainly due to involvement of intricacies in the matter of premium fixing and possibility of payments concerning frequent claims to acutely flood prone areas. Crop Insurance has a large scope and needs to be propagated for adoption by farmers in developing countries.

Types of Floods

There are basically three types of floods, namely flash, river and coastal floods.

Flash Floods : Such floods that occur within six hours during heavy rainfall and are usually associated with towering cumulus clouds, severe thunderstorms and tropical cyclones or during the passage of cold weather fronts. This type of flood requires rapid localized warning system and immediate response in favour of affected communities. Other causes of flash floods include dam failure or other river obstructions.

River Floods : Such floods are caused by precipitation over large catchment areas or by melting of snow or sometimes both. They take place in river systems with tributaries that may cover or drain large geographical areas and encompass many independent river basins. These floods are normally build up slowly or on seasonal basis and may continue for days or weeks as compared to flash floods. There are certain factors such as ground conditions like moisture, vegetation cover, depth of snow *etc* and size of the catchment basin that govern the amount of flood covering the main river.

Coastal Floods : As greenhouse gases warm the earth's atmosphere, sea temperatures will rise, causing the world's oceans to expand and occupy more space. Increase in melting of snow and ice in hills add to amount of water in oceans. This process is already underway. In last 100 years, the tides have crept up by an average of around 20 centimeters. Sea levels are expected to rise upto 44 centimeters by 2080. Due to storm surges during cyclones/hurricanes, three million people are made homeless due to coastal flooding every year. Many low lying countries whose mean height is less than 7 metres are likely to submerge. They include Bangledesh, Japan, Austria, Holland and in India parts like Mumbai, Mangalore, etc. Cost of constructing dykes/ walls to protect the coastal land is prohibitive (US$ 14000 per meter). Developing countries can ill afford it.

Fig. 3.2 : Floods in Plains

Preparedness Against Floods

General. Management and control of adverse consequences of floods require coordination and effective responses systems at centre, state, district and local levels. The neighbourhood community is always the first responder and as such trained and equipped DM teams, consisting of local people should be setup in flood prone areas. All response activated should be accordinated through a suitably devised incident response system under the Collector/District Magistrate. The corporate sector and NGOs should be motivated in making available resources at their command. After the floods recede prompt and efficient medical response to be organised by emergency medical teams. Within the overall DM plan of the State, there should be emergency response plan for each district, involving required measures to be taken before the onset of floods, during the floods and post flood management. Essential components of flood preparations by various agencies are given in succeeding paras.

Fig. 3.3 : Effects of flood in a village

By Department Concerned

- Pre monsoon inspection of all railway tracks, canals and drains by respective departments which include silt clearance from seasonal rivulets.
- Regular clearance of the drains from silt and weeds to make drainage system fully functional and restoration of natural drainage blocking roads, railway tracks and canals.
- Regular maintenance of embankments of rivers, canals, distributaries *etc* and check the canals and siphons.
- Clearing of storm water and sewerage system and free flow drains in towns and cities, before monsoons.

- Constitution of committee comprising of district administration head, heads of all emergency services, medical, police, fire & emergency services, transportation, irrigation, water works, electricity, public relations, civil defence, home guards, NGOs, volunteers *etc*. to ensure proper coordination during the crisis.

By the State and District Administration

- Review of Disaster Management Plans.
- Updation/modification in plans, if deemed necessary.
- Updating DM directory.
- Coordination with designated NDRF, Army/Air Force/Navy/ Para Military Forces units. Exchange of telephones and liaison officers.
- Positioning of flood fighting equipment, like sand bags, boats, out boat motors, inflatable lighting towers, water purifying hand pumps, supplies *etc* at appropriate places.
- Coordination with non government organisations/community based organisations/volunteer organisations.
- Review of situation and visit to likely places for evacuation to ensure their functional availability.
- Make people more aware of the warning and dissemination mechanism.
- Carryout periodic mock drills with all stake holders participating, atleast twice in a year.
- Formulate and circulate Dos and Don'ts for general awareness of public.

Community Participation

Participation from farmers, professional societies, industrial institutions, gram panchayats, women educationalists, urban and rural dwellers and voluntary organizations/NGOs in mitigating flood disaster should be encouraged. The area of participation are flood fighting performances, and response to disaster, including SAR, first aid, relief etc.

Response Mechanism

- On receipt of warning of impending disaster, warn people through print and electronic media, through official channels, through community radio and from religious places.

- District Administration to use local means like loudspeakers, cable network, PA equipment of religious places and dak runners, to inform people, where print/electronic media is not reachable.
- Evacuation plan to shift people to safer predesignated places (higher elevation) like schools, panchayat house, private designated houses. Evacuation drills should be known to people and rehearsed. People should carry their family emergency kits while evacuating. Evacuate cattles too.
- Provide food, safe drinking water, hygiene & sanitation and medical facilities in relief areas/camps. Cater first aid and food for evacuated animals.
- Responsibility for security of houses being abandoned and belongings left behind is that of police and the community. Rather than evacuating complete household the people should be encouraged to anchor their belonging to the ceilings of sturdy houses.
- Local search and rescue teams should be formed for rescuing people from fallen/damaged houses and evacuating them to safer places and administering medical treatment. If evacuation by local teams is not feasible, central search and rescue teams of the district, state and NDRF are pressed into service. If need arises armed forces, are called for rescue by boats, helicopters from marooned places, rivers and water bodies.
- Provide food (cooked/uncooked) and clothing in relief camps, if established. Costly items likes utencils; blankets etc. to be given as per family strength in ration card.
- Once calamity is over, help people restart their livelihood, compensating to an extent for loss of life and property.

Damage Assessment

- Damage assessment is the responsibility of district/local administration, who will cover all aspects of private as well as public properties, including loss and /or damage to crops. The first damage assessment should be sent at the earliest. It must be authentic and reliable. Based on this first assessment relief is arranged at higher levels.
- Inventory of such a detail, before central search and rescue teams are pressed into service if need be, is made with estimated cost of

damages and sent to State Govt. who will release funds from Calamity Relief Fund (CRF), as per prescribed norms.

- If CRF is not able to meet the requirement, the Central Govt. is approached for additional funds. Union Ministry of Home Affairs would depute a Central Team consisting of experts from concerned ministries to make assessment of damages and come to their own conclusion for amount of relief fund to be released. The central team makes presentation to High Level Committee, comprising of Agriculture, Home and Finance Ministers, Deputy Chairman, Planning Commission & Vice Chairman, NDMA, who then approve the relief amount. Based on HLC approval, Finance Ministry release the funds.

Post Flood Management

- Speedy restoration of road traffic, rail routes and postal services.
- Normalise water supply in the affected areas either by arranging tankers or by providing water purifying pumps.
- Repair of the power, telephone and sewerage lines on priority basis so that normalcy is restored.
- Proper continuing arrangements for supply of food, shelter and clothing to the marooned people.
- Ensure adequate supply of petrol, oil, lubricants and kerosene oil to keep the supply line moving.
- Constitution of a survey team of revenue department of district to assess the loss and compensation to be given to the affected population.
- Assistance for repair/rebuilding of private properties, as per the disaster relief manual team's as assessed by district team's.
- Desilting and dewatering of the inundated areas.
- Taking appropriate measures according to Disaster Management Plan for the agricultural sector.

Standard Operating Procedure (SOP) for administration and individuals, pre, during and after the floods are given at Appendices 'A' and 'B' (Pages 31 and 34) respectively.

appendix contd...

APPENDIX 'A'

STANDARD OPERATING PROCEDURE FOR ADMINISTRATION

Pre-Flood Arrangements

- Convene a meeting of the District Disaster Management Authority. It consists of Deputy Commissioner/Collector as Chairperson, Zila Pradhan as Vice Chairperson and members being SSP/SP, district medical officer, district fire officer, municipal commissioner and ADM as member secretary, to review the arrangements. It is recommended that NDRF, SDRF and local Armed Forces representatives be coopted as invitee members;
- Check composition and functioning of the district emergency operations centre;
- Closure of past breaches in rivers and canal embankments and guarding of weak points;
- Rain-recording and submission of rainfall reports;
- Communication of gauge-readings and preparation of maps and charts;
- Dissemination of weather reports and flood bulletins issued by the Meteorological Centres, Central Water Commission, Flood Forecasting Organisation;
- Deployment of boats, sand bags, telephone etc. at desired points;
- Use of power boats at strategic stations;
- Installation of temporary police wireless stations and temporary telephones in flood-prone areas;
- Arrangements for keeping telephone and telegraph lines in order;
- One set of 5 WLL radio sets to be kept as reserve. Encourage use of HAM radios;
- Storage of food in vulnerable, strategic and in key areas;
- Arrangements of dry food stuff and other necessities of life; initially centrally cooking and later by families themselves.
- Arrangements of keeping the drainage system desilted and properly maintained;

- Agricultural measures;
- Health measures; vaccination, keeping requisite medicines in enough quantity etc.
- Veterinary measures; evacuation of cattles, first aid for injured, water and food arrangements
- Selection of flood shelters; elevated and safe areas
- Advance coordination arrangements for NDRF and army assistance
- Training in flood relief work; operating boats, swimming, deep diving, etc.
- Organisation of flood disaster management teams, like SAR, first aid, security, evacuation, etc.
- Other precautionary measures; and
- Alternative drinking water supply arrangements, by purifying flood water through water purification pumps etc.

Organising Rescue Operations During Floods

- Organising enough DM parties to rescue the marooned people within a reasonable time limit;
- Organising shelter for the people in distress. In case the efforts of civil authorities are found inadequate, NDRF, Army, Para Military Forces assistance may be requisitioned;
- Relief measures by non-official and voluntary organizations may be enlisted as far as possible;
- Organise relief camps;
- Provision of basic amenities like drinking water, sanitation and public health care and arrangements of cooked food in the relief camps;
- Making necessary arrangements for air dropping of food packets in the marooned villages /areas through helicopters;
- Disposal of dead bodies and animal carcasses;
- Establish alternate communication links to have effective communication with marooned areas;
- Organising controlled kitchens to supply cooked food initially at least for 2-3 days;

- Organising cattle camps, if necessary and provide veterinary care, fodder and cattle feed for the affected animals for atleast 2-3 days;
- Grant of emergency relief to all the affected people as per state Relief Manual;
- Submission of daily situation reports to SDMA, MHA & NDMA and disseminate correct information through mass media to avoid rumours;
- Rehabilitation of homeless;
- Commencement of agricultural activities – desiltation, resowing;
- Repairs and reconstruction of infrastructure facilities such as roads, bridges, embankments, resettlement of flood prone areas;
- Health measures; (first aid at site, at relief camps, evacuation by ambulances by air and creating surge capacity in hospitals.
- Relief for economic reconstruction.

Post Flood Management

- Sprinkle bleaching powder and lime to disinfect flooded areas.
- Speedy restoration of roads, rail routes and the postal services;
- Normal water supply in the affected areas either by arranging tankers or providing water purifying hand pumps;
- Repair of power, telephone and sewerage lines on priority basis;
- Proper arrangements for the supply of food, shelter and clothing to the marooned people;
- Ensuring adequate supply of POL and kerosene oil to keep the supply line moving;
- Constitution of a survey team by revenue department to assess the loss and compensation to be given to the affected population;
- Assistance to people in getting insurance claim, who have taken 'crop' and 'house' insurance; encourage people to take insurance;
- Assistance for repair/rebuilding of private properties; and
- Desilting and dewatering of the inundated areas.

appendix contd...

APPENDIX 'B'

STANDARD OPERATING PROCEDURE FOR INDIVIDUALS

Before Floods

- Find out if you live in a flood prone area and identify earthen irrigation, hydro electric systems including dams, which are up stream in your area and could be source of potential threat/risk problem;
- Know the terms 'Flood Watch, 'Flood Warning' and 'Urban and Small Stream Warning';
- Don't restrict natural flow of river course by development activities;
- Construction of plinth made of pucca masonry and spread foundations;
- Don't use clay and sun dried bricks without treatment;
- Don't make doors and windows from wood in flood prone areas;
- Important buildings like industrial or commercial structures should not be built in flood prone area;
- Prepare family emergency kit, essential items like portable radio/ transistor, torch, spare batteries, drinking water and dry ready to eat food, first aid box with essential medicines, ORS, match boxes, candles *etc*. before monsoons to last for atleast 3 days per individual; keep family documents like education certificates, land, legal, marriage papers in another bag. These two bags to be kept in safe place.
- Turn off power and gas connections before leaving your homes/ houses.
- Keep hurricane lamp, dragen light, ropes, rubber tubes, umbrella and bamboo sticks in your house.
- Keep your valuables in safe place like bank lockers, including 'Gramin banks'.
- If there is a flood , move along with your family members and cattle to safe areas like relief camp, evacuation centres, elevated grounds.

- Take steps to construct flood shelters. Call your local disaster management office for information; and
- Encourage for insurance policies and keep your household inventory in a safe place.

During Floods

- Listen to radio, local radio or television for local information;
- If local authorities issue a flood warning, be prepared to evacuate;
- Teach health and safety needs to all members of your family; how to turn off the electricity, water, gas supply if you have to leave the house;
- Secure your home, if time permits, essential items to be located outside the house, or secured under the ceiling of the house;
- Stay away from flood water; Do not allow children to play in or near the flood waters
- Stay away from sewerage line, gutters, drains, culverts etc.
- Stay away from electrical poles and fallen powerlines to avoid getting electrocuted
- Do not use wet appliances - get them checked before use
- Be careful of snakes; snakebites are common during floods
- Eat freshly cooked and dry food. Keep food items covered
- When deep flooding is likely, permit the floodwater to flow freely into basement of your house, to avoid structural damage to the foundation of the house;
- Do not attempt to drive over flooded roads. The depth of water is not always obvious. The roadbeds may be washed out under the water and you could be stranded or trapped
- Use boiled and filtered drinking water
- Keep all drains autters near your house clean.

After Floods have Receded

- Stay away from moving floodwater. Moving floodwater six inches deep can sweep you off your feet;
- Stay away from fallen power lines and report to concerned authorities;

- Continue listening to the radio for assistance;
- Consider you health and safety needs. Wash your hands frequently with soap and clean water in case you come in contact with floodwater; Use boiled and filtered drinking water.
- Throw away food that has come in contact with floodwaters;
- Lock all outside doors and close properly windows if you have to leave the house;
- Prevent dangerous pollution - move all insecticides away from the water;
- Best protection during floods, leave the area and take shelter on higher ground along with live stock and farm animals, movable goods and vehicles;
- Adopt the habit of 'Living with Floods'.
- Stagnation of water can breed vector/water borne diseases.
- Use bleaching powder and lime to disinfect the suroundings.

☛ Take People away from Floods, Not Floods away from People.

case study contd...

Case Study

Assam Floods 2004

Brief History of Floods in the State

45 percent of Assam's total area is prone to floods and major reason is river Brahmputra-the longest river that transverse through the state. It originates in Tibet in the North and its outfall is in Bay of Bengal in South. It flows through a total length of 918 km in India, of which 720 km lies in Assam plains itself.

The State of Assam comprises of Brahmputra Valley with 22 districts and Barak Valley with 5 districts, including two hill districts - Karbi Anglong and North Cachar hills. The length of the river Brahmputra valley is 640 km. In the valley, the river Brahmputra is joined by about 20 major tributaries on its north bank and 13 on its south bank. The precipitation here is mainly due to south-west monsoons, heavy rainfall occuring in the months of June - September. Average rainfall in this valley ranges from 1750 mm in Kamrup district to about 6400 mm in the north east hilly regions. Annual rainfall in the state is 1662.2 mm.

In the north eastern region of the State, river Barak is the second largest river originating from Nagaland and Manipur and after traversing for a length of 532 km in India, it outflows into Bay of Bengal after flowing through Bangladesh. The valley is narrow and its width varies from 25 km to 30 km. The maximum discharge of this river was recorded as 6282.64 cusec on 12 August 1989 at Annapurna Ghat.

In 1996, floods in Assam damaged 7848 dwellings, killing 38 people. In 1999, more than 200 villages were inundated and 0.27 million people in 749 villages of 10 districts were affected. In 2000, 1,94,382 people in 12 districts and 483 villages were severely affected. Rail and road communications were cut off in many districts. 3 million people lost their homes and vast stretches of paddy were swallowed by floodwaters. In 1998, the devastation caused by the floods surpassed the extent of damages caused in 1996. An area of 0.972 lac hectares and a population of 46.98 lac were affected. The total damages assessed were around Rs. 700 crores. During 2002 floods, 41 people lost their lives, 19827 houses were damaged and 0.3 million hectares of cropped land was affected. In 2003 floods, 30 people lost their lives, 4600 houses got damaged and 0.2 million hectares cropped area was affected. 7566 villages with population of 5651,954 were affected and 52 lives were lost. 7400 houses were damaged and total damage assessed was Rs, 1,128 crores. The above statistics show that floods have been almost annual feature in Assam.

2004 Floods

Incessant rains since last week of June 2004 throughout the State of Assam and adjoining states of Arunachal Pradesh, Meghalaya, Nagaland and Bhutan resulted in floods in rivers Brahmputra and Barak and their tributaries. One characteristic of this flood was the sudden rise in water levels due to release of waters from dams, reservoirs and artificial lakes within and outside the country. It was first time in history that floods were sustained in one wave for such a long time and affected all the districts of the Assam State. The sustained water level of Brahmputra and Barak rivers above the danger levels for an unprecedented length of time, coupled with 76 deaths, 172 relief camps, 186162 inmates in these camps and the fact that all 27 districts were affected are indicative of the enormity of the disaster. In the rescue plan, the state machinery, Army, Air Force, the para military forces and special disaster management teams of CISF worked day and night to mitigate the sufferings of the people in distress. The Government machinery and the society both faced the crises courageously.

The floods caused widespread damage to human life and property, standing crops, flood control embankment and other basic infrastructure. The Kaziranga National Park was affected. A no. of hog deers, calfs, rhinos, tigers, elephants, wild boars and pythons were reported killed. The national parks of Manas, Orang and Dibru-Saikhowa alongwith wild life sanctuaries Burha Chepori, Pabitora Laokhowa and Bamodi were all affected.

A NGO coordination meeting was held where all stake holders participated and assured fullest help. They were asked to help in their areas of specialisation. The central team for damage assessment carried out their assessment. Installation of hand tube wells, sanitation drives, distribution of water purifying tablets, ORS, spraying of phenyle, bleaching powder and DDT were taken on priority by Administration at district level, particularly in relief camps. Medical relief after checkups intensified. Medical camps were organised by the Army through 12 columns in six districts.

Assam Floods 2004 at a Glance

No. of districts affected 27

No. of villages affected 10,425

Loss of Life 253

Loss of Livestock 29,666

Houses damaged (fully) 5,72,413

Total population affected 1,21,73,969

Total crop area affected .... 12,47,845.17 hactares

Total area affected .... 28,46,979 hactares

Relief Camps 182

Inmates in relief camps 1,86,162

Total hand tubewells sunk 3655

Total medical teams deployed 255

Loss of agricultural land (due to erosion) .... 7,829.72 hactares

Road Network

Loss of agriculture land due to change in river course - 4244.09 hactares. Bailey Bridges were installed to link the remote affected areas for smooth relief work.

Rail Network

Rail communication was however restored slowly.

Govt. of India Response

- Provided helicopters at Guwahati, Tezpur, Dibrugarh, Jorhat and Silcher. They carried out 123 sorties
- Central Govt. released Calamity Relief Fund of Rs. 412.6 million. In addition Rs. 550 million was released from National Calamity Contingency Relief Fund (NCCF).

- Petroleum Ministry released 400,000 litres of kerosene oil.
- Health Ministry sent a central team to advise the Assam State to prevent outbreak of epidemics.
- ISRO sent a team of communication specialists for establishing terminals
- Central search and rescue teams of CISF were deployed for rescue.
- Govt. of India constituted a high level committee to examine all aspects to find a permenant solution to floods in Assam.

All State Level

- State level Disaster Management Committee presided over by the Chief Minister monitored the situation on daily basis
- Flood Management Committees were constituated at State, District and Sub Division levels, to streamline relief works. State Control Rooms started functioning round the clock
- For preparing district reconstruction plan, district level committees consisting of Deputy Commissioner of District as Chair-person and MP, MLAs, Zila Parishad Chairpersons / head of Deptt. as members were constituted.
- NGO coordination was done by having a coordination committee headed by a senior bureaucrat.
- Coordination of assistance from armed forces was carried out.
- Food stuffs, drinking water, medicines, fodder, veterinary care were distributed / given.
- 22 HF and 44 VHF sets were made available for communiction.
- Food inspectors were directed to inspect markets to ensure rotten fish / meat is not sold.
- Rapid action teams of Health Deptt. were deployed for preventive and curative measures.

NGOs : UNICEF provided large amount of medicines. Royal Danish Embassy gave Rs. 23 lac for Sonipur Distt. ACTIONAID provided professional help. USAID, Indian Red Cross also provided aid in advanced warning and restoration of dykes in the breached portion in all the rivers. Permanent solution like raising of bunds was discussed.

A town severely being hit by flood

People trying to save themselves from being drowned

People moving to safer places

Lessons Learnt / Recommendations

- Brahmputra brings a lot of silt in its journey in Tibet and deposit in its course in Assam. Due to silting, its depth keep decreasing. For permanent solution, periodic desilting is required, which is costly.
- Raising the bund of the river near habitations.
- Identifying flood prone areas and not allowing habitation there. Migrants from Bangladesh generally occupy flood plain areas and are worst affected.
- India Meteorological Department to give adequate warning on adjoining areas in China, Myanmar and South East Asia, for better appreciation and preparadness for floods and landslides.
- Central Water Commission to set up control stations with doppler radars, to predict possible rainfall which will help in preparadness and timely evacuation, where required.
- A disaster warning network through earth stations in affected areas linked to central hub at Guwahati, on the modal of Andhra Pradesh may be set up.
- Periodic aerial surveillance generated information will also be of immense help for preparedness.
- Disaster Risk Management Program for all districts of the State.
- SDMA and DDMA, to convene meeting of concerned departments before monsooms, to check on state of preparedness.
- NDRF teams to be deployed in pro-active role before monsoons. They would provide general awareness and capacity development programs, in non disaster period.

case study contd...

Case Study

Peerchu Lake - A Disaster

Peerchu is a river which flows in Tibet. Some years back there was a huge land slide in between two hills which resulted in the blockage of the flow of water. This area is an isolated area, 15-20 km inside Tibet where no habitation exists. As the local administrtion was also not able to oversee outstretched barren uninhabitated land, no one came to know about the landside. The flow of water was blocked and a lake was formed slowly. During winters this area gets frozen and hence some strength was inherently provided to the landslide area which has now became a temporary dam. If the rain fall is less, no effect can be seen. However in 2004, there was sharp rise in the level of water in Sutlaj river, which flows through Himachal Pradesh. It damaged a number of bridges and also threatened the Power Station and other infrastructures on its bank. When efforts were made to find the cause of the rise in water level, including air reconnaissance, it came to light that an artifical lake had been formed in Tibet and if the dam (temporary) was to burst it could create flood sitution not only in Himachal Pradesh but right upto Punjab State.

The Chinese authorities were contacted, who agreed to look into the matter but did not allow Indians to come upto Peerchu lake for detailed analysis. What the Chinese did is not known but the danger of the dam burst still lingers. The fears were not unfounded. In June 2005, again there was breech in the Peerchu lake, resulting in sudden increase of water level from 10 feet to 40 feet in Sutlej River. This resulted in flash floods in Himachal Pradesh and though there were no fatal casualties, property and intrastructure worth Rs. 700 crore were damaged. A number of tourists, including foreign tourists, were stranded and had to be evacuated by IAF (Indian Air Force) helicopters. The situation stabilized but it could perpetuate again anytime without much notice.

Possible Solutions

- The Chinese authorities could be approached to allow Indian specialists to have a detailed analysis. On granting permission take one of the following measures.
- To effect an organised breach in the dam to drain the water. This breach has to be done with precision after detailed calculations
- To strengthen the dam with solid/liquid, easy to carry / helidrop material. This is a long process, costly but feasible.
- To take the dam construction material to the site and convert the present temporary dam into a permanent one. Electricity could also be generated, after the concrete dam comes up.
- During dry season, deepen the lake to take additional water alongwith strengthening the dam.
- Take precautionary measures and remove all infra-structure along the Sutlej in Himachal Pradesh. There will be capital loss.
- To let it remain like this and respond as & when there is a breach.
- A satellite watch on the site should be kept 24 x 7 x 365 days.
- Request the Chinese authorities to divert the water of lake in their area. India could help with monetary and technical support.

Chapter 4

Drought

Introduction

Drought is temporary reduction in water or moisture availability significantly below the normal or expected amount for a specific period. This condition occurs either due to inadequacy of rainfall or lack of irrigation facilities, unexploitation or deficient availability for meeting the normal crop requirement in the context of the agro-climatic conditions prevailing in any particular area. This has been scientifically computed as Moisture Index (MI). Drought in this context can be defined as adverse MI or adverse water balance which may be attributable not only to a prolonged dry spell due to lack or sufficient rainfall but also due to such other factors as excessive evapo-transpiration losses, high temperature, low soil holding *etc*. The inadequacy is with reference to the prevailing agro-climatic conditions in any particular area. For example, there will be drought in Jaisalmer (Average yearly rainfall 200 mm) if rainfall is not sufficient to grow grass and paltry coarse grains, whereas in Bolangir or Koraput in Orissa (yearly rainfall above 1000 mm) there is drought if there is not enough rainfall for bringing the paddy crop to maturity.

Types of Drought

Meteorological Drought : Situation where there is reduction in rainfall for a specific period (days, months, season or year) below a specific amount (long term average for a specific time).

Hydrological Drought : Involves a reduction in water resources (stream flow, lake level, ground water, underground aquifers) below a specified level for a given period of time.

Agricultural Drought : is the impact of meteorological/hydrological drought on crop yield.

Three types of droughts are completely different and are not synonymous.

Rainfall

Indian sub continent experiences average rainfall of around 1200 mm which is well comparable to any country of its size and magnitude. However problem lies in its distribution across the country, which is as under:

a) 33% - Low Rainfall Region 750 mm

b) 35% - Medium Rainfall Region 751-1125 mm

c) 24% - High Rainfall Region 1126-2000 mm

d) 8% - Very high Rainfall Region >2000 mm

Because of erratic behaviour of rainfall, even medium region can be vulnerable to drought conditions. Approximately 2/3 of the country's arable area is at one time or other susceptible to drought. Most of major states like Bihar have both drought as well as high rain areas, due to absence of well developed irrigation system. Any delay in onset of monsoons causes worry at Centre and State level which start contingency plans for shorter term alternative crops. National Commission on Agriculture in 1976 felt monthwise rainfall had greater relevance than rainfall for entire season. Many a times overall precipitation in the season has been normal but the uneven distribution over the months create adverse effect. Good rains in later half of the season (Aug-Sept.) even after drought in first half of the season (June-July) can considerably retrieve the situation. However, failure of rain in later half of season, particularly at maturity stage is invitation to disaster. Whereas floods are a sudden visitation, often coming without much warning, drought are a creeping phenomenon, with hope still lingering till the last stage.

1987 drought was one of the worst of the last century in India. A Cabinet Committee on Drought was set up, which formulated action plan and closely monitored its implementation. The Action Plan emphasized on following:

- Employment generation.
- Provision of drinking water.
- Fodder availability.
- Supply of essential commodities.
- Drought proofing as drought mitigation measures.

Identification of Drought Prone Areas

The Hanumantha Rao Technical Committee on Drought (April 1994) formulated the criterion which is currently in use. The Committee worked out a Moisture Index (MI) to assess the extent of aridity, which broadly speaking is ratio between the precipitation received and the water requirement of the plants under the given agro-climatic conditions. The MI of 300 stations in various regions of India is available on monthly and annual basis. The zoning on this basis by the Committee is as follows:

Table 4.1 :

Moisture Index	Climatic Zone	Percent Area
-66.7	Arid	19.6
-66.7 to -33.3	Semi-Arid	37
-33.2 to 0	Dry Sub Humid	21.1
0 + 20	Moist Sub Humid	10.2
+ 20.1 + 99.9	Humid	7.8
> + 100	Pre Humid	8.3

As per committee report except for Punjab and Kerala, other parts of the country are prone to drought in one year or the other.

Drought Management

Drought by its very nature partakes of crisis management. Success depends on one's ability first to predict and then to control. The strategy for this management is three fold as follows:

- Close monitoring of emerging drought scenario so as to develop an advance warning system.
- Relief measures required for providing immediate succour to affected population and the upkeep of cattle wealth. If possible, to integrate it with long term objectives.
- Coming with an alternative crop strategy for maximum possible retrieval of Kharif crop and a better ensuing Rabi crop.

Fig. 4.1 : Effect of drought on vegetation

Fig. 4.2 : Effect of drought on animals

Warning and Dissemination

Weather Watch Group in Ministry of Agriculture in India meets every week to take stock of the rainfall progress, its effect on the crops from sowing to harvesting during Kharif season. Weekly inputs from India Metrological Department (IMD) give an early warning about the impending drought. States are accordingly informed as and when symptoms of drought are known.

National Agricultural Drought Assessment and Management System has been developed by Ministry of Space for the Department of Agriculture and is primarily based on, monitoring vegetation status through National Oceanic and Atmospheric Administration Advanced Very High Resolution data. The drought assessment is based on a comparative evaluation of satellite observed green vegetation cover of a district in any specific time period with that of any similar period in previous years.

Gujarat State in India, which is an endemically drought prone state has developed a sophisticated monitoring system. The day to day rainfall data from taluks along with IMD data is being converted into a management information system. The water level in each of 105 main reservoirs in the State, the additional inflow of water in these reservoirs during preceding 24 hours and loss of water, if any, either through evaporation or through spill over is relayed to the Central Control Room through wireless stations. Based on this data, decision to drastically cut down or regulate releases of water for irrigation purposes is taken and available quantity of water is released for drinking purposes.

Measures for Combating Drought

- Judicious use of limited irrigation water.
- Rain water harvesting
  - Roof top rainwater harvesting
  - Nadis
  - Tankas
  - Khadins, insitu rain water harvesting.
- *Management of Underground Water :* Recharge underground water by way of infiltration tanks, check dams, injection wells etc.

- *Improved Agronomic Practices :* Quality seeds, use of chemical fertilizer and pesticide to increase production.
  - To retain precipitation insitu and minimise the runoff.
  - To reduce evaporation in relation to transpiration.
  - To use drought tolerant crops that fit the rainfall pattern.
  - To recycle the runoff water after rainwater harvesting and drainage.
  - To use integrated water-shed approach for maximizing rainwater use.
  - To adopt drip farming.

Alternative Crop Strategy

The water availability in 47 major reservoirs in the country is checked at the commencement of most critical period in January/ February. If the IMD also predicts less rainfall, alternative crop strategy is implemented in different states by providing extra power, getting seeds for alternative crops and fertilizers. The farmers are informed before hand and advised for alternative crops. Seeds and fertilizers are given on subsidized rates. This helps in possible retrieval of Kharif crop and a better ensuing Rabi crop, if rains came in later half.

Employment Generation

Generation of additional employment through labour intensive works, like desilting dried ponds, and constructing tankas for rain water harvesting. The projects, which can be taken up on short notice, should be kept ready by District Administration before the monsoons each year. A paradigm of relief-cum development would be more appropriate. Governments National Employment Guarantee Scheme for Families below poverty line, creates employment which has long term development effect.

Drinking Water

With the implementation of Rajiv Gandhi National Drinking Water Mission and Accelerated Rural Water Supply Programme, vast network of water supply schemes have been set-up in the entire country. Provision of hand pumps accounts for bulk coverage of the above schemes. However, their repair and maintenance is a major problem for which village community must assume greater responsibility. Another problem is hamlets (dhanis and majras) or group of houses situated 1-3 km from village and acting as sub village. 30% of population in Rajasthan State in India live in hamlets whose women folk have to cover 2 to 5 km distance daily to get water. Some other ways of supplying water for drinking are :

- In urban areas dig more bores, provide water tankers, trains, if required.
- Continuous monitoring of rural and urban water availability in drought affected areas.
- Preparing a water budget for each irrigation reservoir covering drinking water, Kharif and Rabi requirements and capping damage to ground water regime.
- Undertake repair of tube-wells, where necessary. Repair teams to be ready to move at short notice. Prevent over exploitation of and damage to ground water regime.
- Regulating supply to water intensive industries, if necessary.
- Minimizing evaporation losses in tanks and small reservoirs by using chemicals.

Health and Public Health Measures

People should be accustomed to live on rationed water. This should be taught in schools. However nutritional requirement of all children, expectant loctating nursing mothers should be taken care of Disinfect drinking water sources to prevent spread of water borne diseases and plans to cope up with likely epidemic. Immunisation and surveillance of public health measures be taken.

Cattle Care

Cattles are most affected during drought. It may not be possible to supply fodder or take medical care of individual cattles, however cattle camps on village basis can be opened to take care of complete cattle population. Some other measures are:

- Assessment of fodder requirement on district basis in affected area and import fodder from outside state/country.
- Monitor prices of fodder in selected market places.
- State Forest Department to arrange for cutting and bailing of grass in the forest.
- Fodder cultivation to be encouraged.
- Ensure supply for molasses to cattle feed plants.

Household Strategies for Managing Drought

Special Network : A key strategic aspect for affected households is social network. Families with a large and influential social network are in a better position to negotiate and promote their interests. However, who solicit a favour today must be able to return it tomorrow. A household that does not respect this rule risks being excluded from the network. Consequently poor households are often marginalised.

Diversification of Agropastoral Production : It helps to minimize the potential risks linked to climatic hazards or economic and social crises. In accordance with their resources, households invest simultaneously in rainfed and irrigated agriculture. Horticulture and tree growing are two other areas of investment. An important role is played by livestock which include poultry for small ruminants and for the wealthier households, cattles and horses. Specialized activities like bee-keeping, mushroom farming are recommended for certain households.

Creation of Additional Source of Income : The processing and valorisation of farm products, alongwith crafts, small scale commerce, tourist accommodation, transport services, ambulance services, and seasonal jobs are main opportunities that enable households to reduce their dependence on water. **Investments in the processing of farm products such as wool generate income and diminish the risk of high dependence on water.**

Investments in innovation for rational water use : Farmers invest modest sums and find appropriate solutions. For example, they use perforated PET bottles filled with water and buried between two plants to supply the roots with water in an economical and targeted manner. Another example consists of adding clay to the soil where trees are planted. This reduces the need for irrigation water. **Clay added to holes for tree planting diminishes the need for irrigation water by 40%. Drip farming is being increasingly used to conserve water and yet get high yields.**

Research, Innovation and Exchange of Ideas

The Central Asian Mountain Partnership (CAMP) has carried out research to have better understanding of the strategies adopted by different types of households. The results serve as basis for planning support activities. CAMP supports communities in their village level planning. A number of villages have formed the Central Asian Mountain Village Alliance, an organization that facilitates the exchange of experiences and helps the communities advocate shared interests.

Testing Appropriate Strategies : A household strategy simulation game offers participants a fascinating exercise. They form groups representing fictitious households and invest in various activities, thus developing their strategies. In the course of the game, unexpected events put the chosen strategies to test. At the end of the fictive year, households that have succeeded in generating sufficient income can make new investments and refine their strategies. The simulation game makes it possible for participants to learn more about available natural resources and market opportunities and how to make the most of them, as well as how to minimize risk by diversifying production technology and activities in various sectors. By developing positive synergies between activities they discover opportunities to generate substantial added value.

Conclusion

With modern methods of cultivation and continued good monsoons, the droughts are now becoming rare. However, we must be prepared to face them and hence the need to understand them.

Chapter 5

Earthquakes

How An Earthquake Occurs

An earthquake is a violent shaking of the earth's crust due to breaking and shifting of rocks, beneath the earth's surface. It is believed that our planet earth was formed five billion years ago, from very hot gases, that over a period cooled and became denser. While solidifying, the earth got divided into three distinct layers as illustrated below (Fig. 5.1).

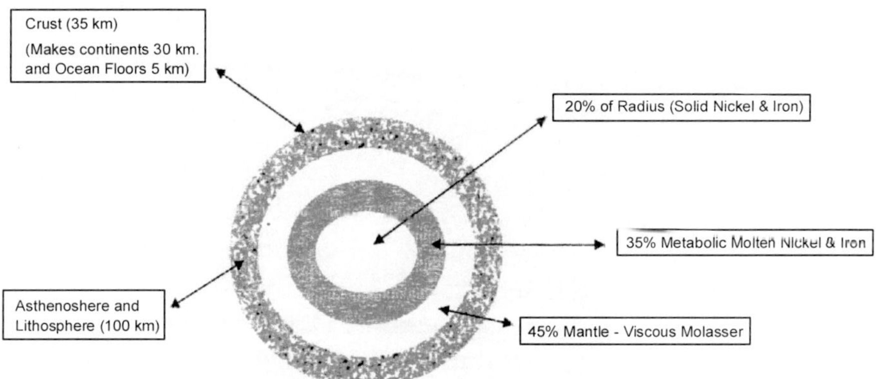

Fig. 5.1 : Composition of Earth

The inner most central part (20% of earth's radius) consists of solid nickel, surrounded by a larger portion (35% of earth's radius) which is molten metal and remaining 45% is mantle of rock with a viscous like material. This mantle part is surrounded by Asthenosphere and Lithosphere. Lithosphere is outermost layer of earth, 100 km thick, top part of which is crust that makes continents and ocean floors. Thickness of crust is around 30 km in continental part and 5 km under the oceans. Lithosphere is chipped or cracked like egg shell and is termed "tectonic plates", which float over the viscous, semi liquid, molasses like structure or mantle. In our planet earth there are 7 large and 12 small such plates which are in continuous motion though this movement is very very slow.

The plates move along three distinctive types of boundaries, that is:

- *Convergent Boundary:* Where plates push each other and one plate slides down the other one.
- *Divergent Boundary:* Where plates pull away from each other
- *Transform Boundary :* Where plates slide past each other.

These are illustrated below:

The Earthquake: Causes

Rocks are made of elastic material and elastic strain energy is stored in them during the deformation that occurs in the Earth. But the material contained in rocks is also very brittle. Thus when the rocks along a weak region on the earth's crust reach their strength, a sudden movement takes place there (Fig. 5.2-3); uneven opposite sides of the fault (a crack in the rocks where movement has taken place) suddenly slip and release the large elastic strain energy stored in the interface rocks. For example, the energy released during the 2001 Bhuj Earthquake was about 300 times (or more) than that released by the 1945 Atom Bomb dropped in Hiroshima.

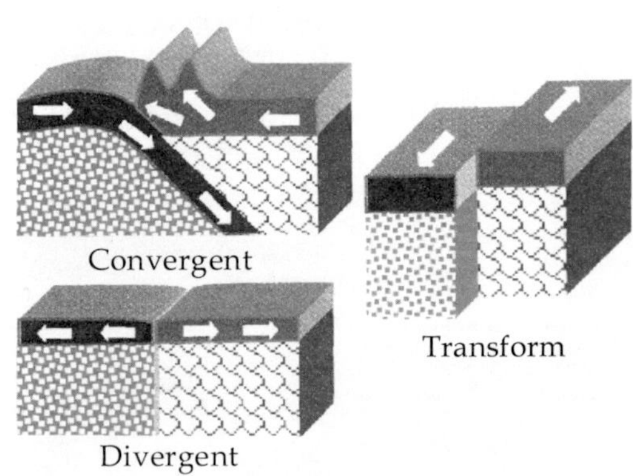

Fig. 5.2 : Types of Inter Plate Boundaries

The sudden slip at the fault causes the earthquake -Violent shaking of the Earth where large elastic strain energy is released and spreads out through seismic waves that travel through the body and along the surface of the earth. After the earthquake is over, the process of strain builds up at this modified interface between the rocks and it starts all over again (Fig. 5.4). Earth scientists term this as the Elastic Rebound Theory. The material points at the fault over which slip occurs usually constitute an oblong three dimensional volume-with its long dimension often running into tens of kilometers.

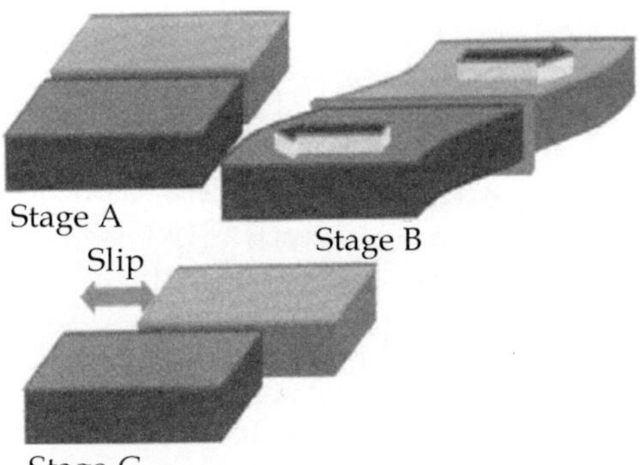

Fig. 5.3 : Elastic Strain Build up and Brittle Rupture

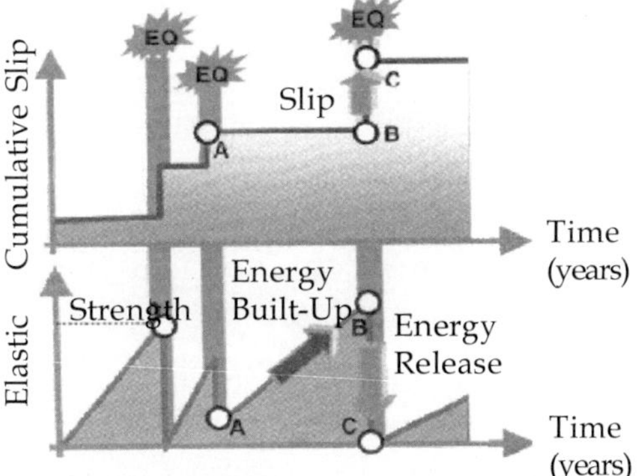

Fig. 5.4 : Elastic Rebound Theory

Types of Earthquakes and Faults

About 95% of all earth-quakes in the World occur along the boundaries of the tectonic plates and are called Interpolate Earthquakes (e.g. 1897 Assam earthquake). A number of earthquakes also occur within the plate itself, away from the plate boundaries (e.g. 1993 Latur earthquake); these are called Intra plate Earthquakes. In both types of earth-quakes, the slip generated at the fault during earth-quakes is along both vertical and horizontal directions (called Dip Slip) & lateral directions (called Strike Slip) (Fig. 5.5), with one of them dominating sometimes.

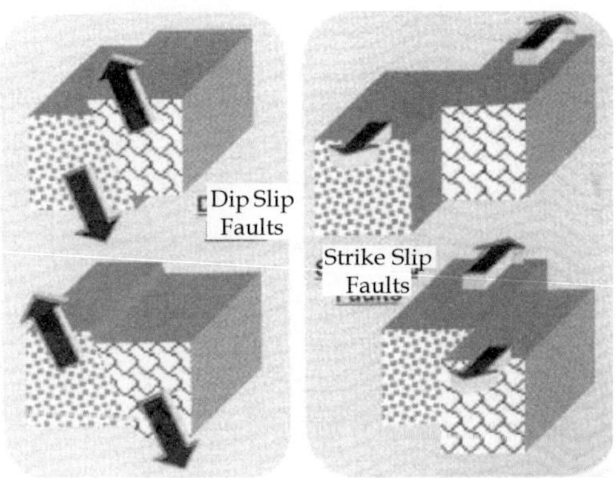

Fig. 5.5 : Types of Faults

How the Ground Shakes

Seismic Waves

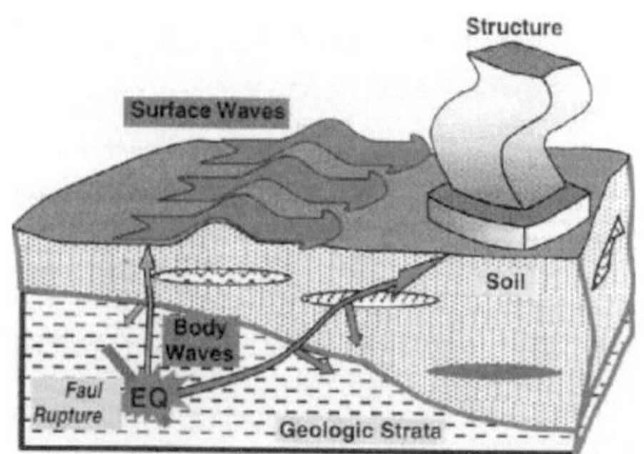

Fig. 5.6 : Seismic wave arrival at a site

Large strain energy released during an earthquake travels as seismic waves in all directions through the earth's layers, reflecting and refracting at each interface. These waves are of 2 types - Body Waves & Surface Waves; the latter are restricted to near the Earth's surface (Fig. 5.6). Body Waves consist of Primary Waves (P-waves) and Secondary Waves (S-waves) and Surface Waves consist of Love Waves and Rayleigh Waves. Under P-waves, material particles undergo extensional and compressional strains along direction of energy transmission, but under S-waves, oscillate at right angles to it (Fig. 5.7). Love waves cause surface motions similar to that by S waves, but with no vertical component. Rayleigh waves make a material particle oscillate in an elliptic path in the vertical plane (with horizontal motion along direction of energy trans-mission).

P Waves are fastest, followed in sequence by S., Love and Rayleigh waves. S waves do not travel through liquids. S waves in association with effects of Love waves cause maximum damage to structures by their rocking motion on the surface in both vertical and horizontal directions. When P and S waves reach the earth's surface, most of their energy is reflected back. Some of this energy is returned back to the surface by reflections at different layers of soil & rock. Shaking is more severe (about twice as much) at the Earth's surface than at substantial depths. This is often the basis for designing structures buried underground for smaller levels of acceleration than those above the ground.

Strong Ground Motions

Shaking of ground on Earth's surface is a net consequence of motions caused by seismic waves generated by energy release at each material point within the three dimensional volume that ruptures at the fault. These waves arrive at various instant of time, have different amplitudes and carry different levels of energy. Thus, the motion at any site on the ground is random in nature with this amplitude and direction varying randomly with time. Large earthquakes at great distances can produce weak motions that may not damage structures or even be felt by human beings. But, sensitive instruments can record them. This makes it possible to locate distant earthquakes.

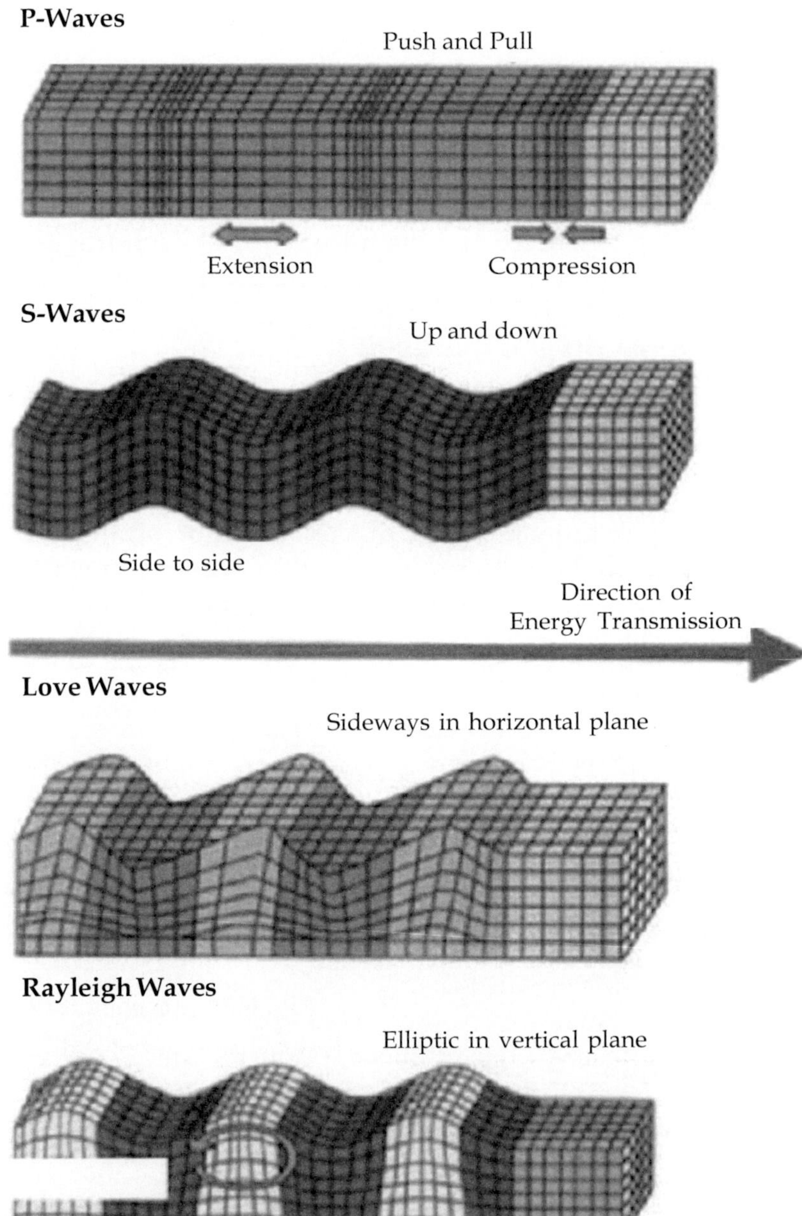

Fig. 5.7 : Motions caused by Body and Surface Waves

Characteristics of Strong Ground Motions

The motion of the ground can be described in terms of displacement, velocity or acceleration. The variation of ground acceleration with time recorded at a point on ground during an earthquake is called an accelerogram. The nature of accelerogram may vary depending on energy released at source, type of slip at fault rupture, geology along the travel path from fault rupture to earth's surface, and local soil. They carry distinct information regarding ground shaking; peak amplitude, duration of strong shaking, frequency content (e.g. amplitude of shaking associated with each frequency) and energy content (i.e. energy carried by ground shaking at each frequency) are often used to distinguish them.

What is Magnitude and Intensity

The point on the fault where slip starts is the focus or hypocenter, and the point vertically above this on the surface of the earth is the Epicenter (Fig. 5.8). The depth of focus from the epicenter, called as Focal Depth, is an important parameter in determining the damaging potential of an earthquake. Most of the damaging earthquakes have shallow focus with focal depths less than 70 km. Distance from epicenter to any point of interest is called epicentral distance.

A number of smaller size earthquakes take place before and after a big earthquake (i.e the main shock). Those occurring before the big one are called 'Foreshocks' and the ones after are called 'Aftershocks'.

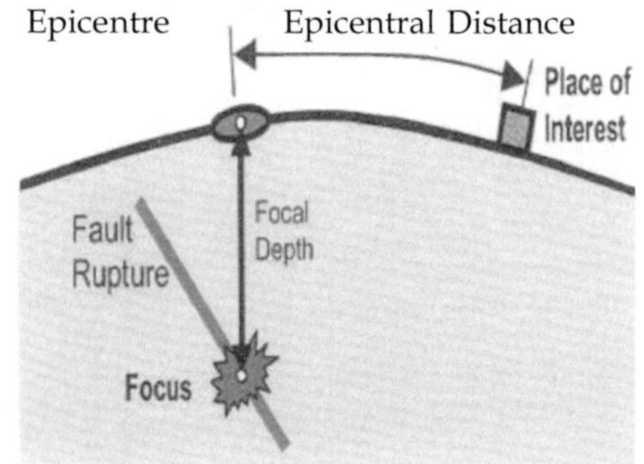

Fig. 5.8 : Epicentre & Focus

Magnitude

Magnitude is a quantitative measure of the actual size of the earthquake. Professor Charles Richter noticed that (a) at the same distance, seismograms (records of earthquake ground vibration) of larger earthquakes have bigger wave amplitude than those of smaller earthquakes; and (b) for a given earthquake, seismograms at farther distances have smaller wave amplitude than those at closer distances. This prompted him to propose the now commonly used magnitude scale, the Richter Scale. It is obtained from the seismograms and accounts for the dependence of waveform amplitude on epicentral distance. This scale is also called Local Magnitude Scale. There are other magnitude scales, like the Body Wave Magnitude, Surface Wave Magnitude and Wave Energy Magnitude. These numerical magnitude scales have no upper and lower units; the magnitude of a very small earthquake can be zero or even negative.

An increase in magnitude (M) by 1.0 implies 10 times higher waveform amplitude and about 31 times higher energy released. For instance, energy released in a M 7.5 earthquake is about 31 times more than that released in a M 6.5 earthquake and is about 1000 (31 x 31) times to that released in a M 5.5 earthquake. Most of the energy released converts into heat fracturing the rocks and only a small fraction of it (fortunately) goes into the seismic waves that travel to large distances causing shaking of the ground enroute and hence damage to structures.

Earthquakes are often classified into different groups based on their size. Annual average number of earthquakes across the earth in each of these groups is shown in the Table 5.1 below:

Table 5.1 : Global Occurrence of Earthquakes

Group	Magnitude	Annual Average Number
Great	8 and higher	1
Major	7 - 7.9	18
Strong	6 - 6.9	120
Moderate	5 - 5.9	800
Light	4 - 4.9	6,200 (estimated)
Minor	3 - 3.9	49,000 (estimated)
Very Minor	= 3.0	M 2-3- 1000/day: M 1-2- 8000/day

Source: http::/neic.usgs.gov/neis/eqlists/eqstats.html

Intensity

Intensity is a qualitative measure of the actual shaking at a location during an earthquake and is assigned as Roman Capital Numerals. There are many intensity scales–two commonly used ones are the Modified Mercalli Intensity (MMI) Scale or MM Scale and Medvedev-Sposheaer-Karnik (MSK) Scale. Both scales are quite similar and range from I (least perceptive) to XII (most severe). The intensity scales are based on three features of shaking – perception by people and animals, performance of buildings and changes to natural surroundings.

Basic Difference : Magnitude versus Intensity

Magnitude of an earthquake is a measure of its size. For instance, one can measure the size of an earthquake by the amount of strain energy released by the fault rupture. This means that the magnitude of the earthquake is a single value for a given earthquake. On the other hand, intensity is an indicator of the severity of shaking generated at a given location. Clearly, the severity of shaking is much higher near the epicenter than farther away. Thus, during the same earthquake of a certain magnitude, different locations experience different levels of intensity.

Intensity has approximately the following relation to the Magnitude:

Table 5.2 : Relationship between magnitude arid intensity

Magnitude	5	6	6.5	7	7.5	8	Richter Scale
Intensity	VI-VII	VII-VIII	VIII-IX	IX-X	X-XI	XI-XII	MMI Scale

Strength of Earthquake

The amount of energy released during different categories of Richter Scale earthquakes are as follows:

Magnitude of Earthquake (Richter Scale)	Energy Released (Amount of TNT)
1.0	170 grams
2.0	6 kilograms
3.0	179 kilograms
4.0	5 Metric Tons
5.0	179 Metric Tons
6.0	5643 Metric Tons
7.0	1,79,100 Metric Tons
7.5	One Megaton
8.0	5,64,300 Metric Tons

Maximum magnitude of an earthquake measured till date is of 9.5 (Richter scale) which struck Chile on 22 May 1960. Sumatara, Indonesia Earthquake of 26 December 2004 was second highest with magnitude of 9.3 on Richter scale.

Modified Mercalli (MM) Scale

The Mercalli Scale modified by the American Scientist describe the effects of an earthquake as given in succeeding paras.

Class of Earthquake

Description

I. Not felt except very few persons under exceptionally favorable conditions.

II. Felt by few persons at best, specially on upper floors of buildings; and delicately suspended objects may swing.

III. Partially noticed indoors especially on upper floors of buildings but many people do not recognize it as an earthquake; standing motor cars may rock slightly and vibration may be felt like the passing of a truck.

IV. During the day felt indoor by large numbers, outdoors by many, at night some may get awakened; dishes, windows, doors disturbed; walls make creaking sound, sensation like heavy truck striking the building; and standing motor cars rocked noticeably.

V. Felt by nearly everyone; many awakened; some dishes, windows *etc.* broken; a few instances of cracked plaster; unstable objects over turned; disturbances of trees, poles and other tall objects noticed sometimes; and pendulum clocks may stop.

VI. Felt by all. Many frightened and run outdoors; some heavy furniture moved; a few instances of fallen plaster of brick buildings of large blocks, half timbered structures and damage to chimneys in stone/clay houses.

VII. Everybody runs outdoors, slight damage like fine cracks in buildings of good designs and reinforced concrete construction; moderate damage in well built ordinary structures; considerable in poorly built or badly designed structures, some chimneys broken; also noticed by persons driving motor cars. In stray cases landslips of roadway on steep slopes; cracks on roads and seams of pipelines.

VIII. Moderate damage in specially designed structures; considerable in ordinary but substantial buildings with partial collapse; very heavy in poorly built structures; panel walls thrown out of framed structures; falling of chimneys, factory stacks, stone walls collapse; heavy furniture overturned and broken; memorials and monuments move and twist, tombstones overturn, changes in well water and disturbs persons driving motor cars.

IX. Heavy damage like large and deep cracks in specially designed structures; well designed framed structures thrown out of plump; very heavy in substantial buildings with total collapse; buildings shifted off foundations; ground cracked conspicuously; and under ground pipes partly broken. Monuments and columns fall. Considerable damage to reservoirs, in some cases railway lines bent and roadways damaged.

X. Some reinforced buildings and well built wooden structures destroyed or totally damaged; most masonry and framed structures with foundations destroyed; ground badly cracked; rail lines bent; landslides considerable along river banks and steep slopes; shifted sand and mud and water splashed over banks. Critical damage to dams and dykes and severe damage to bridges. Underground pipes are broken or bent.

XI. Few, if any, masonry structures remain standing, severe damage even to well built reinforced concrete buildings; bridges destroyed; broad fissures in ground, underground pipe lines completely out of service; earth slumps and landslides in soft grounds; rail lines bend greatly and highways become useless.

XII. Total damage; waves seen on ground surfaces; objects thrown upward into the air. Practically all structures above and below ground are greatly damaged or destroyed. 'Praleh' or total devastation in terms of Hindu mythology sets in.

Medvedev-Sposheaer-Karnik (MSK) Scale

The types of structures, parameters of MSK intensity scale and probable damage to buildings under each stage of scale are given in succeeding paras.

Type of Structures

Structure A: Buildings in field stone, rural structures, adobe houses, clay houses.

Structure B: Ordinary brick buildings of the large block and prefabricated type, half timbered structures and buildings in natural hewn stone.

Structure C: Reinforced concrete buildings and well built wooden structures.

Definition of Quantity

- Single, few - About 5 percent
- Many - About 50 percent
- Most - About 75 percent

Classification of Damage to Buildings

- Grade 1 - Slight damage, fine cracks in plaster; fall of small pieces of plaster.
- Grade 2 - Moderate damage, small cracks in walls, fall of fairly large pieces of plaster, panties slip off; cracks in chimneys; parts of chimney fall down.
- Grade 3 - Heavy damage.

  Large and deep cracks in walls; fall of chimneys.
- Grade 4 - Gaps in walls; parts of buildings may collapse or get separated.
- Grade 5 - Total damage and collapse of buildings.

MSK Intensity Scale

- I - Not noticeable
- II - Scarcely noticeable (very slight)
- III - Weak, partially observed only
- IV - Largely observed
- V - Awakening
- VI - *Frightening:* Damage of grade 1 is sustained in single buildings of Type B and many of Type A. Damage in few buildings of Type A is of Grade 2.
- VII - *Damage to Buildings:* In many buildings of Type C damage of Grade 1 is caused. In many buildings of Type B damage is of Grade 2. Most buildings of Type A suffer damage of Grade 3, Few of Grade 4. In single instances, landslips of roadway on steep slopes; cracks in roads; seams of pipelines damaged; cracks in stone walls.
- VIII - *Destruction of Buildings:* Most buildings of Type C suffer damage of Grade 2, and few of Grade 3. Most buildings of Type B suffer damage of

Grade 3 and most buildings of Type A suffer damage of Grade 4. Many buildings of Type C suffer damage of Grade 4. Occasional breaking of pipe seams. Memorials and monuments move and twist. Tombstones overturn. Stone walls collapse.

- IX - *General Damage to Buildings:* Many buildings of type C suffer damage of Grade 3 and a few of Grade 4, many buildings of Type B show damage of Grade 4 and a few of Grade 5. Many buildings of Type A suffer damage of Grade 5. Monuments and columns fall. Considerable damage to reservoirs; underground pipes partly broken. In individual cases, railway lines are bent and roadways damaged.
- X - *General Destruction of Buildings:* Many buildings of Type C suffer damage of Grade 4, and a few of Grade 5, many buildings of Type B show damage of Grade 5. Most of Type A have destruction of Grade 5; critical damage to dams and dykes and severe damage to bridges. Railway lines are bent slightly. Underground pipes are broken or bent. Road caving and asphalt snow waves.
- XI - *Destruction :* Severe damage even to well built buildings, bridges, water cams and railway lines; highways become useless; underground pipes destroyed.
- XII - *Landscape Changes:* Practically all structures above and below ground are greatly damaged or destroyed.

Can Earthquake be Predicted

Animal Behavior: Can you tell if an earthquake is coming? So far, no; although research in this field is going on in many countries, including in India. Till date, apart from following the old method of watching for clues in unusual animal behavior, the best thing you can do, is just be prepared. However, erratic animal behavior such as frightened or confused pets running around, or a bird call not usually heard at night, could be warning signs. But these are not scientifically proved as yet. However, one should get alert on seeing such abnormal animal behaviour, alongwith other signs.

Ground Water Levels: Sudden change in artesian water levels have been reported prior to an earthquake but this sign cannot be widely applied or depended upon.

Some other known indicators of earthquake prediction are given below:

- 3-4 months before, maximum and minimum tempratures go on rising. On the day of earthquake the temperature may rise as high as 7-12 degrees centigrade.
- 5-7 days before reception of radio shifts.
- 3 days before reception of landline of low quality.
- 10-15 hours before reception of television gets disturbed.
- 10-12 hours before 5-7 times rise in delivery cases.
- 100-150 minutes before, mobile phones mal function/non functional.
- Increase in OPD cases. People become restless, cronic disease symptoms reappear, rise in blood pressure, irritation, headache, migraine, respiratory troubles etc.
- Abnormal behaviour in animals & humans is due to rise in charged particles in the atmosphere.

Indication of an Earthquake: Usually, there is no warning. The first indication of a damaging earthquake may be a gentle shaking. You may notice the swaying of hanging plants and light fixtures, or hear objects wobbling on shelves, or you may be jarred first by a violent jolt (similar to a sonic boom), or you may hear a low (and perhaps very loud/rumbling noise), or a second or two later, you'll really feel the shaking; and by this time, you'll find it very difficult to move from one place to another.

Seismic Zones in India

India lies at the northwestern end of the Indo-Australian Plate – which encompasses India, Australia, a major portion of the Indian Ocean and other smaller countries. This plate is colliding against the huge Eurasian plate (Fig. 5.9) and going under the Eurasian Plate; this process of one tectonic plate getting under another plate is called subduction. A sea, Tethys, separated these plates before they collided. Part of the lithosphere, the earth's crust, is covered by oceans and the rest by the continents. The former can undergo subduction at great depths when it converges against another plate, but the latter is buoyant and so tends to remain close to the surface. When subcontinents converge, large amounts of shortening and thickening takes place like at the Himalayas and the Tibet.

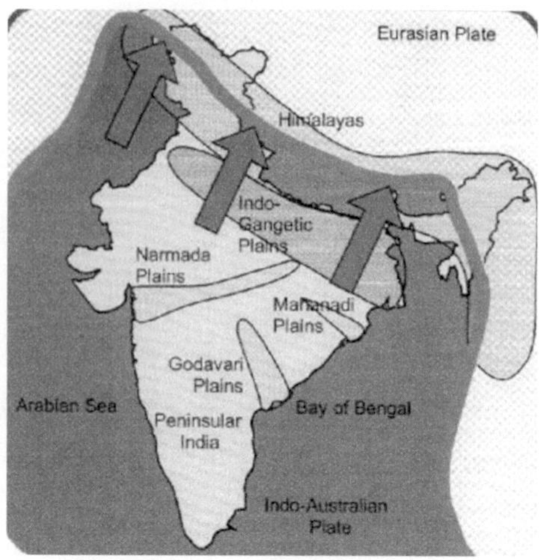

Geographical Layout and Tectonic Plate Boundaries at India

Fig. 5.9 : Tectonic Plates in India

Three chief tectonic sub regions of India are the mighty Himalayas along the north, the plains of the Ganges and other rivers and the peninsula. The Himalayas consist primarily of sediments accumulated over long geological time in the Tethys. The Indo-Gangetic basin with deep alluvium is a great depression caused by the load of the Himalayas on the continent. The peninsular part of the country consists of ancient rocks deformed in the past Himalayan like collisions. Erosion has exposed the roots of the old mountains and removed most of the topography. The rocks are very hard, but are softened by weathering near the surface. Before the Himalayan collision, 40-50 millions years ago, lava flowed across the central part of peninsular India, leaving layers of basalt rock. Coastal areas like Kachchh show marine deposits testifying to submergence under the sea millions of years ago. The impinging of two tectonic plates have yet to end. The Himalayas continue to rise more than one centimeter in a year - a growth of 10 km in a million year! If that is so, why aren't Himalayas even higher? Scientists believe that Euroasian Plate may now be stretching out rather than thrusting up.

Prominent Past Earthquakes in India

A number of significant earthquakes have occurred in and around India in last nearly 200 years. Four great earthquakes (M>8) occurred in a span of 53 years from 1897 to 1950. Each of these and others caused disasters, and a number of lessons were learnt. Scientific publications have warned that very severe earthquakes are likely to occur anytime in the Himalayan Region which could adversely affect the lives of several million people in Indian sub-continent. Details of prominent earthquakes are given below.

Table 5.3 : Prominent earthquakes since 19th century

S/N	Date	Event	Time	Magnitude	Max. Intensity	Deaths (Approx)
1.	16 Jun 1819	Katchchh	11:00	8.3	IX	1500
2.	12 Jun 1897	Assam	16:25	8.7	XII	1500
3.	4 April 1905	Great Kangra	06:20	8.0	X	19,000
4.	15 Jan 1934	Great Bihar-Nepal	14:13	8.3	X	11,000
5.	15 Aug 1950	Great Assam	19:31	8.6	XII	1,530
6.	21 July 1956	Anjar	21:02	6.1	IX	115
7.	10 Dec 1967	Koyna	04:30	6.5	VIII	200
8.	23 Mar 1970	Bharuch	20:56	5.2	VII	30
9.	21 Aug 1988	Bihar-Nepal	04:39	6.6	IX	1,004
10.	20 Oct 1991	Uttarkashi	02:53	6.4	IX	768
11.	30 Sep 1993	Killari (Latur)	03:53	6.2	VIII	7,928
12.	22 May 1997	Jabalpur	04:22	6.0	VIII	38
13.	29 Mar 1999	Chamoli	00:35	6.6	VIII	63
14.	26 Jan 2001	Bhuj	08:46	7.7	X	13,805
15.	26 Dec 2004	Great Sumatra	06:28	9.3	XII	10,749
16.	08 Oct 2005	Kashmir	09:20	7.4	X	1,308

Seismic Zoning Map of India

The varying geology at different locations in the country implies that the likelihood of damaging earthquakes taking place at different locations is different. Thus a seismic zone map is required so that buildings and other structures located in different regions can be designed to withstand different levels of ground shaking. The latest seismic map of India having only four seismic zones – II, III, IV & V, is given in Fig. 5.10 below:

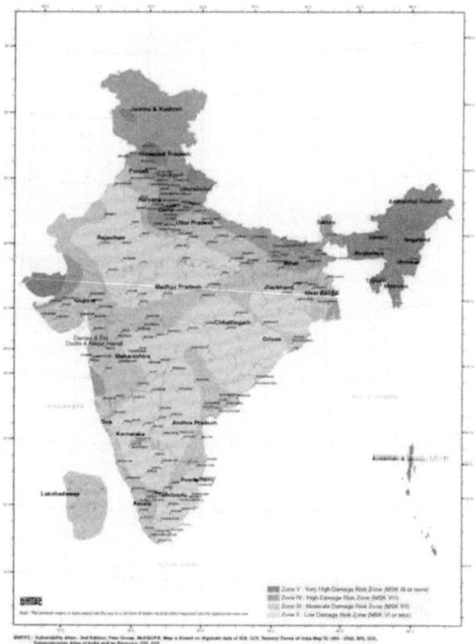

Fig. 5.10 : Seismic zone Map of India

Earthquake Mitigation

As per seismic zone map of India (IS : 1893, 2002) (Fig. 5.10) 58.7 percent of India's land area is vulnerable to moderate or severe seismic hazard, i.e. prone to shaking of MSK intensity VII and above. In the last two decades, most Indian cities have witnessed phenomenal growth of multi-storied buildings, super malls, luxury apartments, modern flyovers as part of process of development. The construction activities in rural areas have also been exponential. It is thus imperative to incorporate seismic risk reduction strategies. While Govt. has taken measures to reduce the risks, the community has a vital role to play which is given in succeeding paras.

Community Based Preparation for Earthquake

The community living in Zone III, IV & V need to be sensitized and prepared for the unpredictable earthquakes. It should be done at the level of block/village/mohalla/colonies by respective disaster management machinery, like resident welfare associations, gram volunteers and NGOs *etc.*

Sensitization of Community

- Check seismic zone you are staying in
- Organise a meeting to discuss earthquake dangers and earthquake response actions at family and local levels.
- At this meeting, all members of the community should be given an opportunity to express and discuss their concerns about personal safety, safety of their belongings and their dwellings. Encourage them to prepare their families to cope up calmly, safely and effectively before, during and following an earthquake, especially if family members are separated when the event occurs.
- Learn about causes and effects of earthquakes, from disaster experts.

Developing a Family Disaster Plan

- First of all get your house surveyed by a structural engineer to find out if it is safe as per the seismic zone, it is located in. If not, get it strengthened through retrofitting.
- Identify safe place in each room of home. Also pick up safe place, in your office, school and other buildings where you visit.

- Discuss about your family disaster plan with your family, neighbours and caretakers.
- All moveable items like almirah, TV, pendent light fixtures, picture frames, mirrors, etc. should be anchored/secured.
- Family disaster plan should include what to do and where to meet your family after an earthquake.
- Identify one relative in another city to provide information about your safety. This person's telephone number should be known to all family members. Telephone numbers of first responders, neighbours, family doctor, nearest hospitals should be known.
- Make two emergency kits, one containing valuables and important documents like land papers, educational, sports, legal and experience certificates and the other kit should contain a torch with extra battery, small fire extinguisher, drinking water, money in cash, portable radio with spare batteries, first aid kit, candles, easy to cook or precooked food items. These kits should be checked from time to time and kept at easily identifiable safe place in the house. Family member who would escort them should be known, including reserve.
- Identify emergency exit with alternative and keep them clear.
- Teach members of your family how to turn off electricity and gas at main switches and valves. Make one or two of them responsible for it.
- Train your family members in 'basic first aid'. Medical facilities are likely to be overwhelmed immediately after a severe earthquake. Training will help you to keep calm and know what to do when an earthquake occurs.
- Hold earthquake drills at regular intervals and ensure maximum presence.

Fig. 5.11 : Objects can fall during an earthquake and injure people. Place large and heavy objects on lower shelves in your home. Make sure that there are no heavy objects hanging above your bed or place where you usually sit.

Fig. 5.12 : Move flower pots off the top of walls and away from the edge of ledges. Flower pots are likely to fall during an earhquake and could injure people.

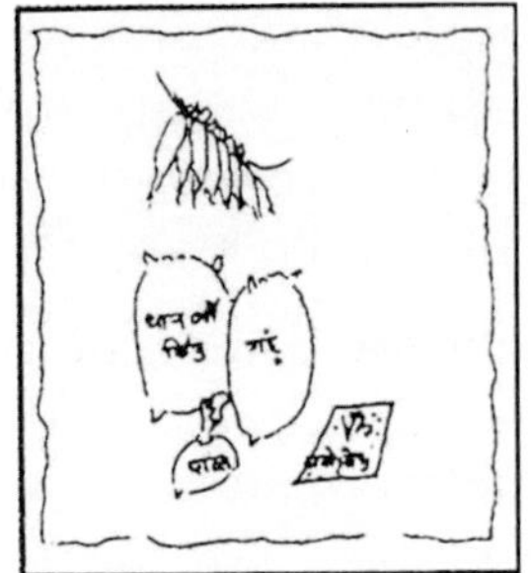

Fig. 5.13 : Farmers should store seeds, grains and vegetables in safe places so that they are available even after an earthquake.

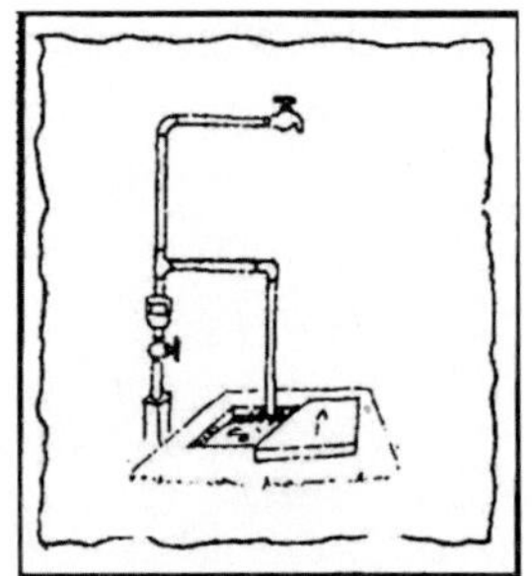

Fig. 5.14 : Water stored in underground tanks is more likely to be available after an earthquake than water stored in tanks on the roof top

Fig. 5.15 : Emergency Kit. It is good idea to store an "emergency kit" in your home with all the supplies you will need if an earthquake, or another disaster occurs. You should store the following items; food and water, adequate for at least one day for your family, battery operated radio with extra batteries, a torch or candles and matches, first aid supplies such as bandages and basic medicines. Store all these items together in a location that should be accessible even if your home is damaged

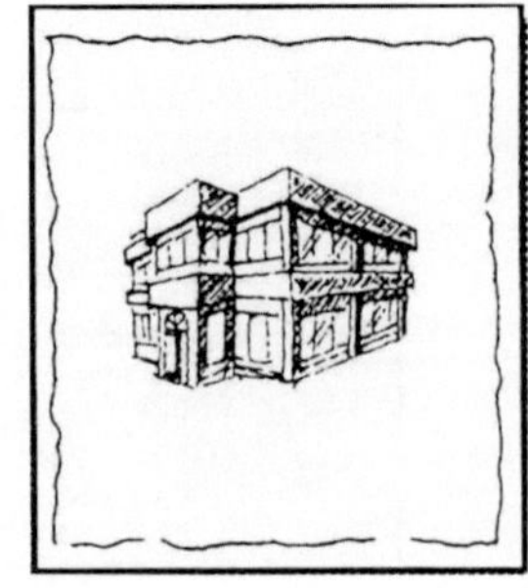

Fig. 5.16 : A house which looks nice from the outside is not necessarily strong inside

Fig. 5.17 : Consider buying earthquake insurance for your house

Fig. 5.18 : Building a seismically resistant house will help keep your family and possessions safe in event of an earthquake happening.

Fig. 5.19 : It costs almost the same amount (only 3-4% extra) to build an earthquake resistant house as it costs to build a non-earthquake resistant house. If you are planning to build a new house, consult architect and structural engineer on how to build your home as safe as possible, as per BIS code.

Fig. 5.20 : If you are inside or near an exit when earthquake strikes, exit the building and find a location far away from buildings, walls, trees, narrow streets and power lines.

Fig. 5.21 : If you are on the upper floors of a building during an earthquake, do not jump from a window or a verandah. Take crouching position under a column and wait until the shaking stops before using the stairs.

Fig. 5.22 : If you are outside when the earthquake strikes, do not go inside a building.

Fig. 5.23 : **Fig. 5.24 :**

If you are outside when an earthquake strikes, go to a location far away from buildings, walls, trees, narrow streets and power lines.

Fig. 5.25 : If you are inside a vehicle when an earthquake strikes, pull over to the edge of the road and stop. Stay away from buildings, trees, power lines and bridges.

Fig. 5.26 : Only use telephones and roads in the first few hours after an earthquake, if it is an emergency. These facilities need to be kept free for use by first responders.

Fig. 5.27 : The first priority of rescue workers after an earthquake is usually to make sure that important emergency facilities are safe, such as hospitals, schools and police station.

Fig. 5.28 : A battery operated radio is usually the best way to get information after an earthquake. Store one in your family kit.

Fig. 5.29 : There will be aftershocks, that is, additional earthquakes after the first large earthquake. Stay away from houses which might be damaged because they may collapse during an aftershock

Fig. 5.30 : After the shaking stops, stay in an open space. Be ready to help rescuers by identifying injured people who need help.

Fig. 5.31 : After an earthquake, do not move people who are injured unless they are in immediate danger of further injury. If it is necessary to move someone, be very careful. You can make someone's injuries much worse by moving them improperly.

Fig. 5.32 : Roads and bridges are often weak after an earthquake. Be cautious if you need to drive heavy vehicles

Fig. 5.33 : Develop a plan for your family to reunite after an earthquake, in case an earthquake occurs when all family members are not together. It is a good idea to select a site near your home and yet away from all buildings, trees and power lines, where everybody will gather.

Fig. 5.34 : Don't stand near the windows

Fig. 5.35 : Don't keep heavy items overhead

Fig. 5.36 : Switch off gas connections

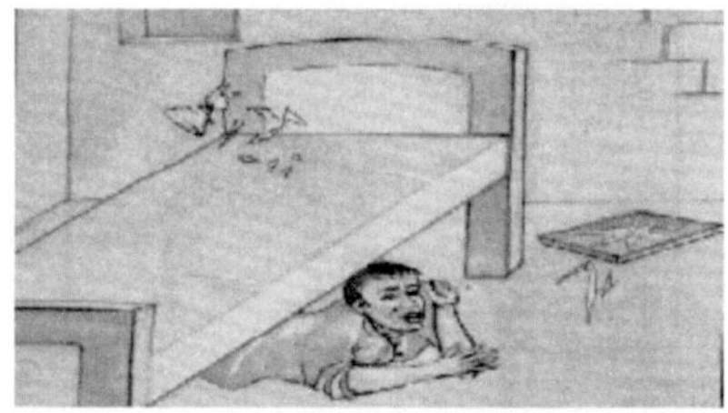

Fig. 5.37 : Take cover under or next to a furniture

Fig. 5.38 : Don't rush out of house during earthquake

Fig. 5.39 : Stay away from electricity lines

Fig. 5.40 : People who volunteer to help the specialist search and rescue teams should be very careful when entering damaged houses. Wear protective clothing and helmet.

Fig. 5.41 : People who know foreign languages other than English can help the relief effort after an earthquake by identifying medicines and supplies sent by non-English speaking countries. Be prepared to enlist help of such people.

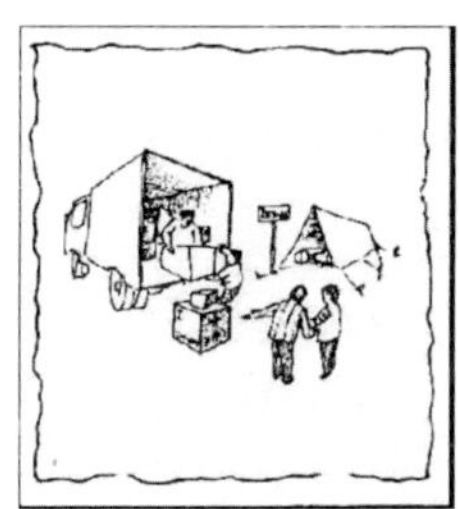

Fig. 5.42 : The procedure to distribute government loans after an earthquake needs to be simple in order to be fair to everyone. It should be as per State Disaster Relief Manual.

Fig. 5.43 : Epidemic disaster spread easily in temporary shelters, if people are not careful about sanitation

Fig. 5.44: J&K earthquake October 2005, has proved traditional buildings made of wood and mortar can withstand severe earthquakes better than concrete buildings.

Fig. 5.45 : Construction of earthquake resistant buildings has been advocated as per NDMA Guidelines.

Fig. 5.46 : Training sessions in earthquake resistant construction should be offered regularly in all engineering colleges and at community level.

Family Kit

There are six basics, you should stock in your home; water, food, first aid supplies, clothing and light bedding, tools and emergency supplies:

a) *First Aid Kit :* Assemble a kit for your home. A first aid kit should include, roller bandages of different sizes, a pack of cotton, small scissor, antiseptic solution (e.g. dettol, savlon), antiseptic cream (e.g. soframycin, neomycin), oral re-hydration solution (ORS), triangular bandages, gauge pieces - small and large, sterilized dressings, small & large splints made up of wood or bamboo sticks, pain killer tablets (e.g. Paracetamol) medicines for loose motions/stomach ache and other prescribed medicines.

b) *Water :* Store drinking water in unbreakable bottles/containers as per minimum daily requirements, two bottles per person/day. Nursing mothers & children need more water. Refill every four months.

c) *Food :* Store non-perishable food items that will not require much maintenance or refrigeration. Select items that are compact, lightweight and according to staple food habits. Some examples are, biscuits, wafers, namkeens, kurkare, ready to eat food that do not require cooking/instant food, dry foods like peanuts, dry fruits, chana, moori, satu etc., sugar, salt, pepper, energy drinks like glucose, glucon-D, special needs of family member (a kid, lactating mothers, ill or elderly), instant coffee, tea bags etc.

d) *Clothing & Light Bedding :* One change of clothing & footwear. Bedding as per season. Items to be carried, bed sheets, blankets/ sleeping bags, canvas shoes and raincoat/umbrella.

e) *Tools and Supplies :* Disposable plates, spoons, paper bags, list of emergency phone numbers in a diary, battery operated radio and extra batteries, torch and extra batteries, disinfectant, chlorine/halogen tablets, utility knife, candle and match boxes, soap, liquid detergent, thread and needles, medicine dropper, whistle, plastic sheets, feminine supplies, personal hygiene items, plastic bags, small ropes for tying or rubber band/personal sanitation, plastic mugs.

f) Special Items

   i) *For Babies :* Powdered milk, diapers, and medications.

ii) *For Adults :* Heart and BP medicines, insulin, denture needs, eye glasses/contact lenses.

iii) *Important Family Documents :* Will, insurance, policy, contracts, deeds, stocks, bonds, election I-card, ration card, passport, bank pass books/cheque books, credit card, degree certificates, birth/death certificates, marriage certificates, legal documents, etc.

How to Protect your Property

- While building your house, make sure it is designed as per Indian Standard Buildings Codes for the area and is safe.
- When laying foundation, go right up to the bedrock level to ensure house is built on firm ground. As far as possible avoid filled up areas.
- If purchasing a house outright, ascertain that the building is earthquake resistant. Consider getting it evaluated by a professional structural engineer. Must get expert advice, if there are signs of structural defects.
- If you are already living in a house/flat, ask your architect/engineer/builder to make your building earthquake resistant. Ensure to improve its safety.
- You can make your building earthquake resistant by Retrofitting. For this consult, qualified structural engineer or architect.
- False ceilings and loose electrical fittings must be properly anchored to avoid economic losses and injuries even during minor earthquakes.
- In a tall multi-storied frame building, if ground floor of your building is open for parking, it has higher probability of damage. Get it checked.
- Check that roof top water storage tanks are properly tied with the main structure. Secure them from falling off.

Do not keep flower pots on parapet wall or sunshades over doors/windows. Secure them, if you have to.

Do's and Don'ts for Individuals / Families

What can you do before an earthquake occurs:

- Follow earthquake resistant building codes for new constructions and insist on earthquake resistant features.

- Ensure that your house is safe : you can strengthen an existing building by getting it retrofitted.
- Do not stock glass or crystal-ware on higher shelves; shake will topple them and break into numerous pieces.
- Anchor overhead lighting fixtures appropriately to check their fall due to seismic vibrations.
- Provide strong support to gas and power appliances.
- Prepare first aid box and learn first aid treatment. A short capsule will help.
- Prepare life saving family kit which include torch, candle, matchbox, blanket, readymade food items, water bottle, medical kits and radio with additional batteries.
- A separate kit should consist of valuables including important documents.
- Family members should know location of electric switches, so that at the time of disaster they can be switched off.
- Train yourself in basic rescue & first aid functions.
- Practice occasionally in the family drop-cover-hold drills. Drop (bend) next to a strong table or between two tables placed next to each other or take crouching position in corner of room, under beam etc.

What can you do during an earthquake?

- If you are in a structurally sound building, stay still there.
- If you are inside an old weak structure, take the fastest way out and prevent injury from falling debris.
- If you are near an exit leave the building. Do not rush to exit point. Get out calmly in an orderly manner.
- If you are not near an exit or in a high rise building stay inside
- Drop, protect your head and take cover.
- Inside a building, protection next to table or other sturdy furniture in triangle of life. Drop cover & hold.
- You should take crouching position close to the floor, or under beam or in a corner.
- Move away from glass window, book shelves and unsecured heavy objects. Also stay away from buildings with glass panes.

- After the shaking stops, switch off all gas, refrigerator, heater, geyser, air conditioner and other electricity appliances *etc.*
- After tremors are over, exit your place and move out in the open area, as aftershocks may occur any time
- Do not push others. It can cause stampede.

If you are in a House

- Don't use lift for getting down from multistoried buildings.
- Do not rush through stairs, when shaking is taking place.
- Be prepared to move with your family after the earthquakes has subsided, taking your two emerging kits.

If you are in a Shop, School, Office or Theatre

- Stay inside
- Don't run for an exit. Stampede could prove fatal.
- Take cover in, 'triangle of life', or in one corner.
- Move to corner or middle of side walls.
- Move away from glass windows, display cases or other obvious hazards.
- Cover your head with your arms and stay calm till the shaking is over. Then move out in an orderly manner.
- Let younger children, elderly and disabled people leave first.
- Do not panic.
- Move away from power lines, poles, walls, false ceilings, parapet, falling flower pots & other elements that may fall or collapse.

If you are in a High Rise Building

- Move away from exterior wall immediately. Cover your head with helmet if available, otherwise with hands.
- Take protection in, 'the triangle of life' space.
- Don't rush for exits.
- Stay in the building until shaking stops.
- Don't use elevator. Use stairs for coming down only after the shaking stops.
- Remain calm and self assured and help others who are distressed.

- Check for fire. Call for Fire Services (101) or Police Control Room (100), or District / State Disaster Control Room, as required.
- If you are on a steep hill side, move away in case of landslides and falling rocks.

If you are Outside

- Avoid high buildings, walls, power lines and other objects that could fall and create block.
- Don't run through streets.
- If possible, move to an open area away from trees, sign boards, buildings, electric wires, overhead high tension transmission cables.

If you are in Vehicle

- Move to side of the road and stop the vehicle.
- Move away from flyovers, powerlines and advertisement boards.
- Jump out of the car and crouch on its side, in 'triangle of life'.
- Do not sit inside the car; it may topple, injuring you.

What can you do after an Earthquake?

- Check for injuries to your family members and other around you.
- First treat yourself then help others. Do not attempt to move seriously injured persons unless they are in immediate danger of further injury/succumbing.
- Remain calm and self assured.
- Check for fire. Call the fire services (101) or Police Control Room (100). Inform District Disaster Emerging Operation Center.
- Check your electricity meter and gas lines for defects. If any damage is suspected turn the system off from the main valve/ switch. Switch off electricity, water and electricity connections from the mains.
- Clean up household for chemical spills, toxic and flammable materials to avoid any chain of unwanted events.
- Listen to radio or watch local TV for emergency information and additional safety instructions.

- Stay out of damaged buildings. Expect aftershocks.
- Leave a message stating where you are going, if you must evacuate residence.

If you are Inside a Building

- Use the telephone or mobile to inform in crisp language, if you are stranded. Do not clutter telephone lines. Leave them free for use by emergency managers/first responders.
- Remain in a safe position until shaking stops.
- Check electricity, water and gas services and turn them off.
- Listen to your radio and watch TV for information and advice.
- Be calm and encourage family members to be patient.
- Be ready to experience aftershocks after the main earthquake.

Try to get out of building after the shaking stops.

- If injured, get treatment at the earliest.
- Turn off the gas connection.
- Do not smoke and do not light matches or use a cigarette lighter.
- Do not turn on switches. There may be leaks or short circuit.
- Use a torch at night and in dark places.
- If there is a fire, try to put it out. If you cannot, call the fire and emergency/services.
- If you know that people have been buried and you could not take them out, inform the rescue teams. Place flags or lights for rescuers to identify location where people are trapped.
- Do not rush and do not worsen the situation of injured persons or your own situation by taking impulsive decisions.
- Avoid places where there are naked electric wires and do not touch any metal objects in contact with them.
- Do not drink water from open container without having examined it and filtered it through filter or an ordinary clean cloth.
- Eat something, You will feel better and more capable of helping others.

- If your home is badly damaged you will have to leave it. Collect emergency kits, one containing valuables and important documents, like land & legal papers, certificates and the other kit consisting of water, ready to eat food, first aid kit, torch, transistor with spare battery and special medicines for persons with heart complaints, diabities, *etc*.
- Do not walk around the streets to see what has happened. Keep clear of the streets to enable rescue vehicles to pass.
- Move to your duty place as given out in community disaster management plan and as practised during mock drills.

Earthquake Mock Drills

- Earthquake strikes without warning, hence, life protecting actions must be taken immediately, at the first indication of ground shaking. There will not be time to think what to do.
- Therefore, of all earthquake preparedness measures, earthquake drills are the most important. Their purpose is to help the community learn how to REACT immediately and appropriately.
- Essential of earthquake drills are discussions, demons-trations and exercises designed to help community learn and practice where to seek shelter and how to protect their heads and bodies from falling objects (*e.g.* debris from ceilings, light fixtures, and shattered glass).

Effective Earthquake Drill Evaluates

- Actions to be taken during an actual earthquake, and
- Actions to be taken after the ground shaking stops.

The Important Components of Mock Drill are to Anticipate

- What dangers to expect during an earthquake?
- What quake - safe actions to take during an earthquake?

Know

- How to conduct drills?
- How to provide first aid to victims?
- How to develop procedures for evacuating the building after the shaking?
- How to practise and evaluate the effectiveness of your earthquake drills?

Development of Procedures for Evaluation of Earthquake Drills

The following earthquake drill is an example of standard response actions to be taken by the community. The complete earthquake drill includes actions to be taken during a simulated earthquake, evacuation after the shaking stops, rescuing victims trapped under debris and providing first aid to injured.

Sample Community Earthquake Drill

During an earthquake drill simulated by sounding of a siren, the community should demonstrate following ability to react immediately and appropriately :

- All should drop and take cover.
- Some should take cover in corner of room or center of side walls.
- Nobody should be seen taking position or standing near a window or under a door.
- Some may take cover near sturdy, furniture like table, elevated bed *etc.*, in triangle of life space.
- All should stay under cover until shaking stops (unit siren stops).
- Some selected persons should be seen switching off electricity, water and gas mains, after the shaking stops.
- All should practice listening to local radio/TV.
- All participants to listen and obey instructors.

Following the Instructor's Command, Community will

- Immediately TAKE COVER next to desks or tables, and TURN AWAY from windows.
- No one runs towards exits.
- All remain in sheltered positions for at least 60 seconds (simulated by siren), (earthquakes do not last more than one minute).
- Simulated casualties will be evacuated.
- After shaking stops, instructors will order evacuation.
- Community DM Teams will be activated for search and rescue of persons under debris, rendering first aid to injured and providing relief etc.
- Observers are detailed and briefed by the coordinator.

During the Earthquake Drill, Coordinator will

- Set off siren at designed time.
- Observers will check duck, cover & hold drill.
- Coordinator will order evacuation.
- After drill conduct debriefing taking inputs from observers and reviewing all actions by different stake holders.

Procedure for Evacuating Buildings

- Building evacuation following an earthquake is imperative due to the possibility of secondary hazards, such as after-shocks, explosions and fires.
- Through repeated drills, the community undoubtedly should demonstrate their ability to exit the building in a quick and orderly manner. It is, however, difficult to estimate how long it will take for the community to manoeuvre through the debris that might have fallen in their path to safety, because surprises lead to confusion and anxiety. Community should be told what to expect and how to navigate safely.
- Evacuation of vulnerable people, like injured, children, families with single woman as head, lactating mothers, children below 5 years, differently abled persons, elderly people etc. should be planned & executed meticulously.
- Emphasize that evacuation takes place only after ground shaking ceases, building evacuation should be practised as an extension of "duck-cover-hold" drills.
- An aftershock may occur while communities are evacuating through a crowded area. Discuss advantages and disadvantages of sequentially evacuating the place through the crowded area. Occasionally practise "duck-cover-hold" along evacuation routes.

Plan for Unexpected

Identify all possible emergencies you might have to handle during an earthquake evacuation and generate alternative response procedures. For example, discuss what to do if:

- The power fails.
- The door jams
- If exit route is blocked – alternate route.

- Hallway and stairway are littered with debris.
- An aftershock occurs.
- There is smoke in the hallway.
- There is small fire due to short circuit.
- Persons are injured and cannot be moved.
- How to carry old, disabled, infirm and small children.
- Contents of the family kits.
- Locate a safe assembly area.
- Ensure assembly area is away from buildings and overhead power lines.
- Is this area away from underground electricity and sewer lines?

Evaluate the Effectiveness of the Earthquake Drill

Use the following checklist to assess the effectiveness of earthquake drill procedures. If you have not, as yet, initiated earthquake mock drills in your community, use the checklist as a guide for developing and conducting meaningful earthquake mock drills.

Earthquake Drill (Simulated Exercise) Evaluation

Assess the preparedness of the community in drill by asking following questions:

- Are all the community members familiar with the "duck-cover-hold" procedure?
- Have all the community members demonstrated their ability to take immediate and correct actions?
- Is there sufficient shelter space, at their home for all family members.
- Do all the community members know how to protect themselves, if no shelter is available?
- Are the community members prepared to remain in quake-safe positions for up to 60 seconds?
- Does the community has trained DM teams, like SAR, first aid, relief teams etc. Activate all DM teams.
- Are the community members evacuated from the buildings to pre selected safe outdoor area following a simulated earthquake?

- ❐ Does your post - earthquake building evacuation procedure consider the very real possibility that strong aftershocks may occur within minutes after the main event?
- ❐ Have the disaster management teams been adequately exercised in performance of their roles?
- ❐ Have the community members been given ample opportunity to discuss their fears and concerns about earthquakes?
- ❐ Have the community members been instructed on how they can help each other and in each phase of earthquake?
- ❐ Is community prepared for various phases and stages of earthquake.
- ❐ Are earthquake drills viewed as an opportunity to discuss earthquake preparedness in each home?

Immediate Response and Care Requirements during an Emergency

A major earthquake will cause widespread damage and may trigger other dangers such as fires and release of hazardous materials from on-site or in-transit containers. Local emergency personnel will be severely overtaxed. It may be several hours before they are able to respond to calls from each place, within the affected community. A record of active emergency responders with their reserves should be kept.

The community's responsibility to ensure the care and safety of children, women, the old persons, the physically disabled during the immediate aftermath of an earthquake is especially critical. First aid must be provided at the earliest. The whereabouts of every such group must be known and recorded. **It will be a good idea to detail teenage children to look after each and every such group member, especially who do not have their own younger able family members with them.** Small fires must be abated before they get out of hand, and utility systems must be secured.

There is no guarantee that specialised response including emergency medical or fire personnel will be able to respond to affected community during the first "critical" or "golden" hour, following a major earthquake.

The community should plan as to how they are going to prepare themselves to carry out emergency response within first 60 minutes.

- How to evaluate staff resources and training needs.
- Discuss among your community, how to facilitate immediate action.
- Anticipate first hour priorities.
- Attend to the first aid needs of injured persons.
- Account for all members of your community.
- Locate missing members of your community.
- Extinguish small fires before they get out of hands.
- Check damage to utility systems and appliances; if necessary, shut off power, gas and water mains. Seal off and indicate areas where hazardous materials have spilled.
- Be calm and reassure frightened personnel.
- Establish communication with emergency assistance officials first responders.

Use of Simulators

Use of simulators could also be made to practise or exercise core members of community/ block/ district/ state. In Japan, they have 'shake tables' which produce vibrations of different intensities to depict earthquake of various magnitudes. School children are made to feel the vibrations at the shake tables.

Providing Medical Assistance

The Common Injuries

Earthquakes can cause a number of injuries, the most common among them are:

- Heart attack.
- Stop breathing/difficulty in breathing.
- Bleeding cuts from flying/broken glass.
- Shock
- Bone injuries
- Trauma cases

The community/family/school/ office/organization, each should have first aid kits.

A first aid kit is an essential part of any emergency kit, especially after an intense regional earthquake. The kit should include the following items to treat injuries that commonly result from earthquakes:

- First aid bandages
- Adhesive strips
- Butterfly bandages
- Roller bandages
- 4 x 4 sterile gauze dressings (individually wrapped)
- Non - allergenic adhesive tape
- Safety pin scissors
- Triangular bandages
- Antiseptic wipes
- Blunt - tipped scissors
- Small plastic cup to wash/rinse eyes
- Thermometer
- Antibiotic solution
- High - absorbency or other disinfectant
- Asprin and acetaminophen
- Medicines for mild stomach upsets, headache, fever.
- Clean and sterilized cotton cloth
- Blanket

Tips to Treat Injuries

If the victim appears to be unconscious

- Tap and shout, "Are you okay? And proceed as follows:
- Open the airway
- Check breathing for 3-5 seconds unless you suspect a spinal injury.
- If there is no breathing, give 2 breaths - 1 - ½ seconds per breath.
- Check the victim's breathing and pulse at the side of the neck for 5-10 seconds.

- If there's a pulse but no breathing and the victim is an adult, give him or her mouth to mouth, one breath every 5 seconds.
- If there's no pulse, try to get medical assistance as soon as possible.

In Case of Bleeding

- Using a sterile dressing or clean cloth, apply firm steady pressure.
- Elevate the wound if you do not suspect a broken bone.
- If bleeding continues, press harder with a new dressing on top of the old one.
- Use instant blood clotting adhesive.

In Case of Shock

- Keep the victim lying down; elevate his/her feet if there is no spinal injury.
- Immobilize injuries such as broken, dislocated or sprained bones with splints or slings, keep the victim quiet.
- Prevent chilling, obtain medical help as soon as possible.

Safety Tip

Common household items that can be used as first aid substitutes include :

- Sheets for bandages
- Rolled up magazines for splints
- Doors for stretchers
- Bamboos with individual clothes as stretchers

Post – Earthquake Evacuation

- Evacuation should NEVER be automatic.
- There may be more danger outside your building or facility than there is inside. Your building may be more safer, if it built as per National Building Code.
- There may be no safe assembly area outside.
- There may be no clear route to get outside, and alternate routes may need to be cleared, which will take time.
- The lighting inside your building or room, will probably be working. Out-side it may be dark.

- ❒ Before any decision is made to vacate your house, someone must find out if there is.
  - A safe route out, and
  - A safe place to assemble.

Look for Potential Post Earthquake Hazards Outside the Building

- ❒ Power lines
- ❒ Trees
- ❒ Areas near buildings that may have debris fallen on them – parapets, roof tiles, chimneys, glass panes.
- ❒ Routes past concrete block walls.
- ❒ Covered walkways.
- ❒ Places under which large gas mains run.
- ❒ Hazardous material storage areas.
- ❒ Designate open areas outside that are without overhead hazards and removed from potential danger spots; choose an off - campus spot such as a park or agriculture fields near the residential area.
- ❒ Assembly areas should be as close to the facility as is safe so that community members have easy access to the daily needs.
- ❒ Everyone of the community should be informed about evacuation plans.
- ❒ Have all your community/family members reviewed the plan.
- ❒ Include all your community/family members with disabilities in the drills and exercises. Earmark persons who will ensure their evacuation.
- ❒ Hold practice drills and exercises two or three times a year.
- ❒ Alternate routes in each drill.
- ❒ Evaluate your drills and exercise and make changes in community DM Plan as necessary.

After the Earthquake Gather Information and make Decisions

Community

- ❒ Do not automatically rush into the corridor or outside the building.

- Assess the intensity or wait to hear instructions from the elders of your family who may have experienced the earthquake earlier.
- Circumstances in which you have to wait a long time without hearing anything, you will have to make decision yourself.
- If you are in an unsafe place (the ceiling has collapsed, wires are crackling, broken glass or chemicals are all over the floor, you smell gas or smoke), you will want to leave, but you must inspect for damages before you move to safety.
- Account for all your family members before you leave the house.
- If the house damage forces you to evacuate, take injured family members with you only if moving them will not cause further injury.
- The lights will probably be out and it may be dark - always have a handy torchlight/flashlight, at your home that works.
- In an aftershock, everyone should duck and take cover until the shaking stops.
- Once you get to a safe location, communicate your whereabouts to the other members of your family by whatever methods you think best (including cellphone/mobile). Contact outside the city/town should be informed.
- Carry out immediate survey and report damages, if any, to concerned government authorities.
- Provide help in clearing of routes for emergency supplies and rescue operations.
- Contact District Collector/District Emergency Operation Centre (EOC) State EOC to undertake relief operation like distribution of rations, clothing, water, medicines and grants.
- Assist in erection of emergency shelters.
- Guard nearby public and private properties.
- Participate in fire fighting.
- Trace missing individuals and take care of children rendered parentless.

Do's and Don'ts for Administration and Relief Volunteers

The following are the do's and don'ts in case of earthquake disaster for relief volunteers and administrators in order to facilitate relief and rescue activities when earthquake strikes.

Before an Earthquake

- Enrolment of volunteers trained for basic first aid instructions and relief and rescue operations. Keep record.
- Assess the magnitude of problem likely to arise. Carry out studies on possible scenarios of future earthquakes, to point out gaps in planning and preparedness.
- Allotment of responsibilities between official and non-official agencies. Coordination of relief and rescue organisations. Identification of search and rescue teams and assistance from defense services.
- Resource evaluation regarding manpower, equipment, transport, hospitals, fire fighting units and so on.
- Inventory of medicine, fire-fighting equipment, portable communication sets under India Disaster Resource Network (IDRN).
- Identify emergency shelter accommodation such as schools and community buildings.
- Ready made designs for appropriate emergency cost effective shelters suitable for the region.
- Management, planning and installation of instruments concerning information and communication network, and make shift communication unit.
- Draw hospital contingency plan. Mobilisation of mobile field hospitals and surgical units to be planned.
- Enforce national and state building codes for new constructions.
- Demonstration of earthquake resistant houses suited to the region.
- Assess vulnerability of structures and retrofit and strengthen weak ones.
- Draw education programs for general masses & school children. Make posters, handouts, films, TV programs, press notes *etc*.
- Train administrators, engineers and masons about earthquake resistant construction.
- Collect technical data about earthquake by suitable instruments.
- Sustained efforts in research and development activity on earthquake resistant design.
- Conduct mock exercises for all contingencies, periodically but atleast twice in a year.

After an Earthquake

- Survey the affected area by collecting number of houses damaged/collapsed, lives and livestock lost, estimate compensation, shelters required, repairs *etc.*
- Prompt operational decisions.
- Assess the emergency needs.
- Report assessed damage and needs to higher authorities.
- Arrangement for proper rescue and evacuation services to victims.
- Procurement measurement/impressment of transport.
- Setting up of Emergency Operation Centre (EOC) in the District which will have information center, search and rescue, media, relief, medical, NGO management NDRF *etc.* stations in it.
- Provide emergency shelter and medical aid.
- Check spreading of rumors.
- Disposal of dead bodies.
- Psychological and traumatic care of victims.
- Restoration of lifelines and essential services such as telecommunication, roads, electricity and water supply.
- Repair/replacement and restoration of damaged structures/ equipment.
- Rehabilitation and reconstruction of new earthquake resistant buildings/structures.

Damage Prevention and Rehabilitation by Retrofitting

Details of how retrofitting of earthern and brick building is done are given in Appendix 'C' (Page 97).

Do and Don'ts while Constructing Houses

Do's and don't's while constructing earthern and brick buildings are given at Appendix 'D' (Page 101).

National DM Guidelines on Management of Earthquakes

NDMA issued National guidelines on management of earthquakes in April 2007. These guidelines are based on six pillars of Earthquake

Management. They envisage institutionalization of stakeholders, initiative by involving communities and other stakeholders, cover the pre disaster components of mitigation and preparedness on scientific and technical principles as well as on indigenous technical knowledge and building techniques. They simultaneously address the incorporation of multi-hazard resistant features in the reconstruction of damaged buildings and outline the strategy for strengthening the post disaster components of emergency response, rehabilitation and recovery. All new structures would be built in compliance with earthquake resistant building codes and town planning by-laws, as a national resolve. The guidelines advocate the need for carrying out the structural safety audit of existing lifeline structures and other critical structures in earthquake prone areas and carrying out selective seismic strengthening and retrofitting.

The guidelines also emphasize the need for strengthening enforcement and regulation, awareness and preparedness, capacity development (including education, training, R&D and documentation) and response. The six pillars mentioned earlier, in brief are as follows:

- Incorporation of earthquake resistant features for construction of new structures.
- Selective strengthening and seismic retrofitting of existing priority and lifeline structures in earthquake prone areas.
- Improve compliance regime through appropriate regulation and enforcement.
- Improve the awareness and preparedness of all stakeholders.
- Introduce appropriate capacity development interventions for effective earthquake management (including education, training, R&D and documentation).
- Strengthen the emergency response capabilities in earthquake prone areas.

appendix contd...

APPENDIX 'C'

DAMAGE PREVENTION AND REHABILITATION BY RETROFITTING

Retrofitting of Earthen Buildings

Generally different types of cracks like vertical, inclined, and cracks at the corners are seen in earthen walls, constructed using mud, unburnt bricks or unburnt blocks. It is also observed that the weak walls separate at the corner, which may cause the collapsing of the house.

For such types of buildings, the following steps are followed for repair and retrofitting:

- Cracks must be fully filled using good clay mortar with fibers as shown in this (Appendix 'C').
- Cracks at the corners or 'T' junctions should be filled as suggested above but before that bamboos shall be inserted between the cross walls at about 75 cm interval above the floor insertion of bamboos, at the corners.
- About 75 mm above the floor on the internal face of the wall, cut a grove about 75 mm x 75 mm and one meter long in each wall.
- Place a bamboo of 40 to 50 mm dia and 1.5 m long in the groove and the hole in both walls.
- Fill the groove and holes with the mud mortars.

In case of shifting of roofing or roofing tiles or falling or breaking of tiles and shifting of rafter, the following steps are followed:

- Roofing tiles should be removed for further work and the rafters should be properly positioned. The opposite rafters should be tied together through horizontal braces. Then after adjusting the bamboo purlines the tiles should be placed back properly to complete the roof.

If there are no earthquake resisting elements in the house, in spite of repairs and restoration, the house will remain weak against future earthquakes. The house is strengthened as follows:

- A seismic band should be provided on top of all inner and outer walls below the roof and the roofing rafters should be attached to this band.

- If the rooms are longer than 5 meter either a cross - wall should be inserted or external or internal buttresses may be added to reduce the length of wall to less than 4.5 meter.
- The height of the wall should be not more than 8 times the thickness. If it is so, the height should be reduced.
- It is preferred to have only one opening either door or window in one wall of about 4.5 m length.

Providing Seismic Bands

- Erect the ridge and the rafters as usual, spiking them to the ridge members. Also tie them to the outer bamboo of the seismic belt using binding wire.
- The opposite rafters on both sides of the ridge should be connected near about mid height of the roof through bamboo ties nailed to the rafters.
- Just below these ties, fix long bamboos across the rafters nailed to all the rafters in the room.
- Near each end of the room, provide cross - bracing using bamboo,which should cover and connect to three or four rafters of each.
- Fix the bamboo purlines on top of the rafters by nails as usual and lay the roofing tiles.

Retrofitting of Brick Buildings

Generally the brick buildings experience different types of cracks like vertical and inclined cracks. Apart from these types of cracks, wall separation is also observed at the corners. Following steps should be followed:

- Cracks must be filled using good cement - sand mortar in ratio of 1: 6 or near cement grout.
- The cracks, at the corners or 'T' - junctions should be filled as above but before that the walls at right angles should be connected using ferro - cement plates.

Methodology for Grouting Cracks

- Remove the plaster near the cracks from inside as well as outside the walls and clean the cracks thoroughly with water and air jet.

- Wet the cracks, if dry, by sprinkling water.
- Fill the cracks in the whole thickness of the wall with neat cement grout in fine cracks and 1: 6 cement - sand mortar in wide cracks. The filling should be done starting from bottom towards top of wall, through port holes made while sealing the cracks from both sides.

Installing Ferro - Cement Plates at the Corners

- Use wire mesh in a width of 450 to 500 mm each side of the crack both inside and outside the room in a depth of 400 to 450 mm at about 900 mm above the floor.
- Second similar connection to be made above lintel level.

The earthquake shaking may also affect the roofing elements. The roofing tiles are seen to have shifted or fallen down and broken, the rafters have also shifted and fallen or broken.

- The roofing tiles should be removed for further work and the rafters should be properly positioned. The opposite rafters should be tied together through horizontal braces. Then after adjusting the bamboo purlines, the tiles should be placed back properly to complete the roof.

If the buildings are not having earthquake resistant features, there may be chances of damage even after the repair work is done in advance. The following steps may have to be followed:

- Check length, height and thickness of walls and modify to conform to the code.
- Check the positions and sizes of openings in walls and modify as required or provide reinforcement.
- Provide seismic bands or seismic belts just below roof and just above door/window lintel level.
- Modify the roof structure by providing additional bracing elements and fix it to the seismic band/belt.

Control on openings in walls

Door and window openings should satisfy the following:

- Distance of jambs from internal corner = 230 mm or more.
- Distance between two consecutive openings = 450 mm or more

- Sum of widths of opening in a wall should be less than 0.37 of the wall length in the room.
- If not, close an opening or reduce its size. Otherwise provide ferro-cement strengthening around the openings.

For the building to behave like a single unit, the best optimal solution indicates the use of seismic belts, at various levels:

- Install a seismic belt on all walls on both sides above lintels of openings and another one just below roof level.
- Height of belt should be between 400 to 450 mm: longitudinal wires in weld mesh 16 of about 2 mm dia at 25 mm c/ c; transverse wires same dia at about 150 mm c/ c; micro concrete 1: 1 : 3 or cement coarse sand mortar 1 : 3 of 30 to 35 mm thickness.
- Remove plaster; rack out mortar joints to 12-15 mm depth: clean surface; wet surface with water; apply near cement slurry and plaster first coat of 12 mm thickness and roughen its surface; fix the mesh with 150 mm long nails at about 450 mm apart while plaster is still green; apply second coat of plaster of 16 mm thickness.

Making the Roof Structure Stiff

- Erect the ridge members and the rafters as usual spiking them to the ridge members.
- Tie the rafters with the seismic belt.
- Connect the opposite rafters on both sides of the ridges near about mid - height of the roof through bamboo ties nailed to the rafters.
- Just below these ties, fix long bamboos across the rafters nailed to all the rafters in the room.
- Near each end of the room, provide cross bracing using bamboos, which should cover and connect to three or four rafters each.
- Fix the bamboo purlines on top of the rafters by nails as usual and lay the roofing tiles.

appendix contd...

APPENDIX 'D'

DOS AND DON'TS WHILE CONSTRUCTING BUILDINGS

DON'TS	DOS
Brick Construction Planning and Layout	
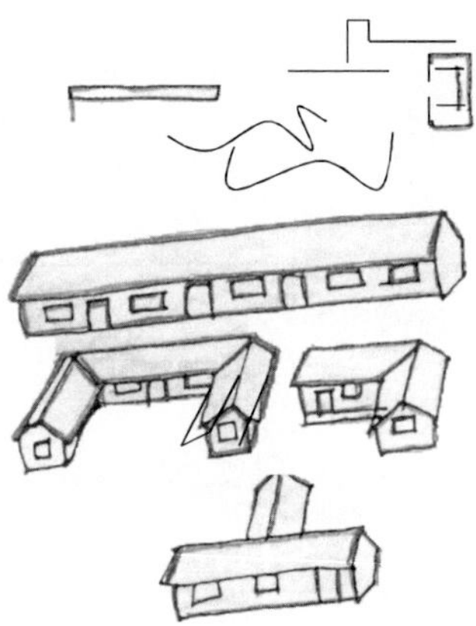	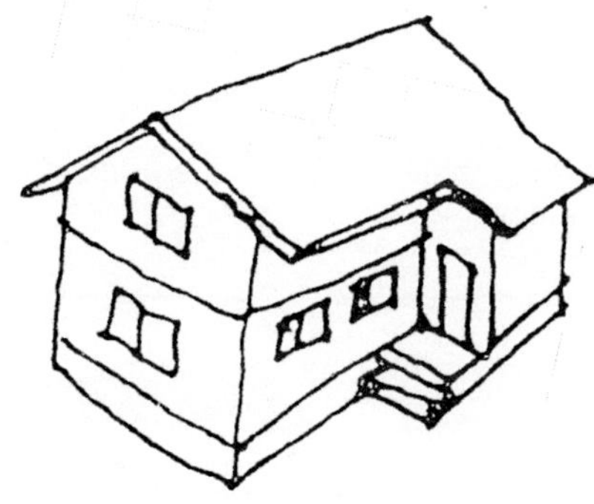
Very long buildings. L-shaped buildings. Zig-zag with attached wing or courtyard are undesirable	Plan should be as simple as possible. Good options are square and round
	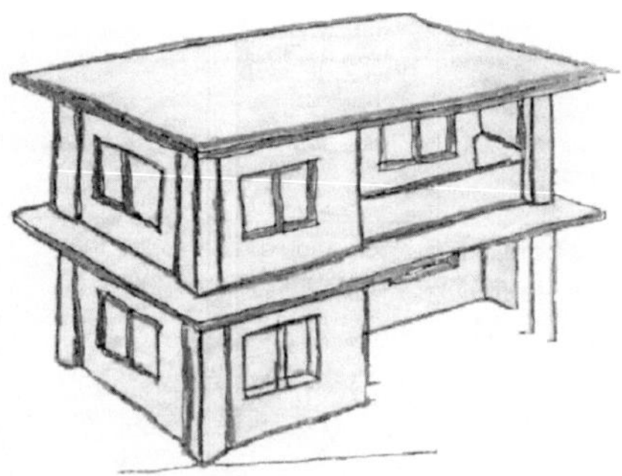
There should not be big difference in height and weight of different parts of same building.	Vertical shape of building also to be very simple, square and uniform in weight.

DON'TS	DOS
 Trees should not be planted adjoining the building walls	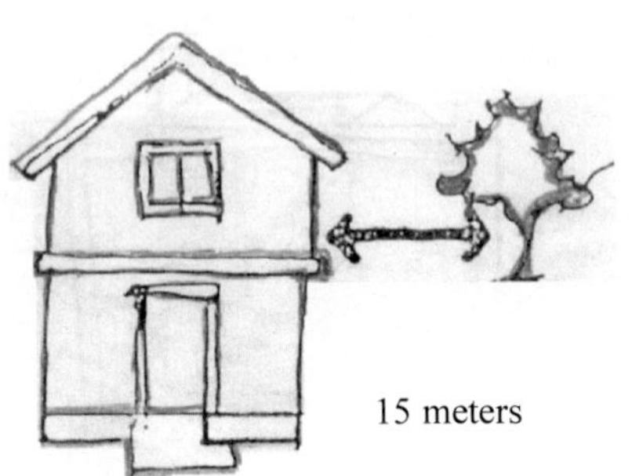 All trees planted should be minimum 15 m away from buildings
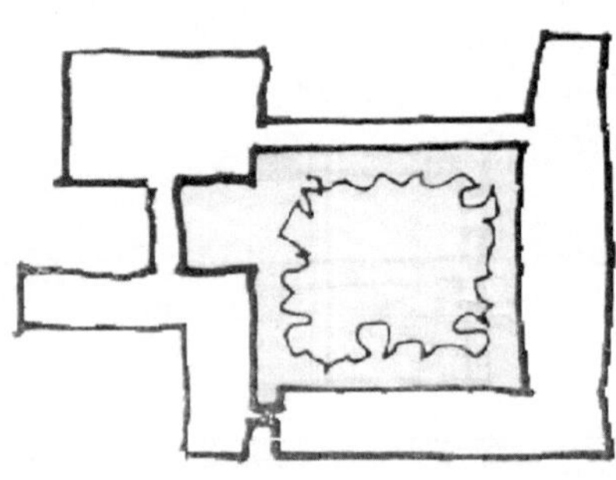  Grouping should not allow collapse of neighbouring buildings.	  The grouping of the buildings should be such that it minimises the risk due to the collapse of one or more buildings on neighbouring buildings and roads.

DOS

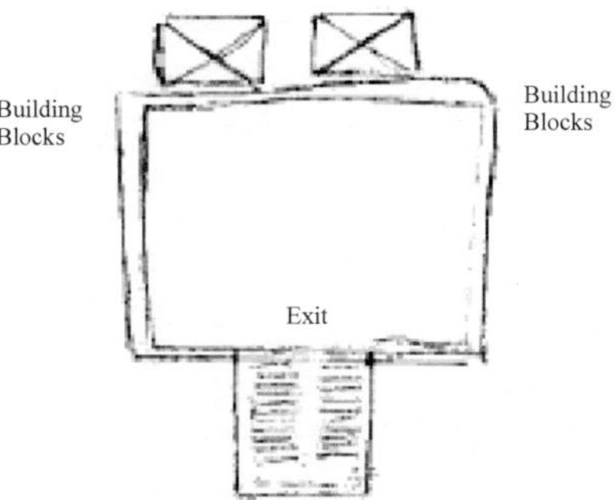

Multi-storey buildings should have more than one staircase.

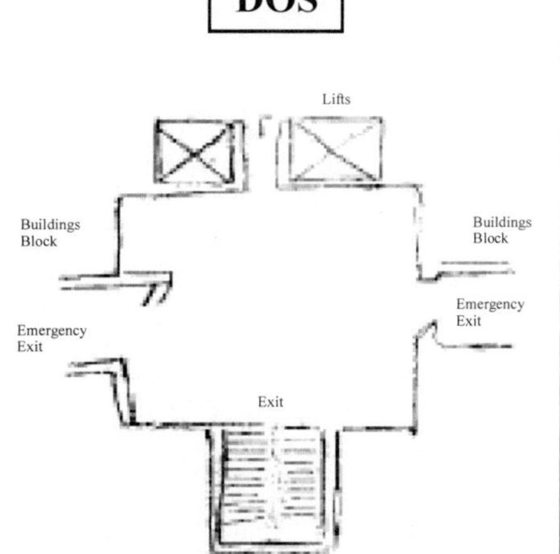

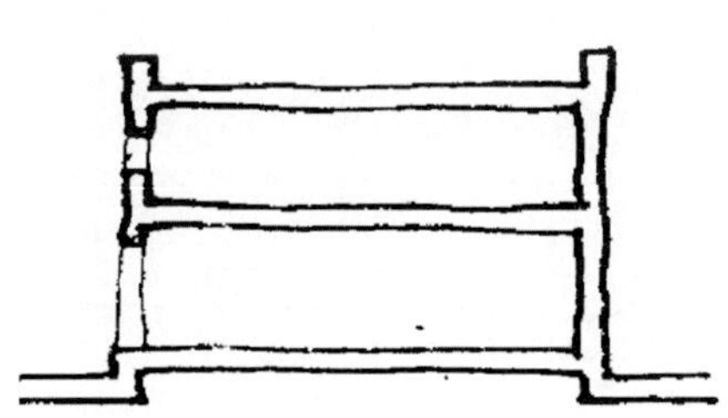

Height (ht) of each storey > 3.2 M

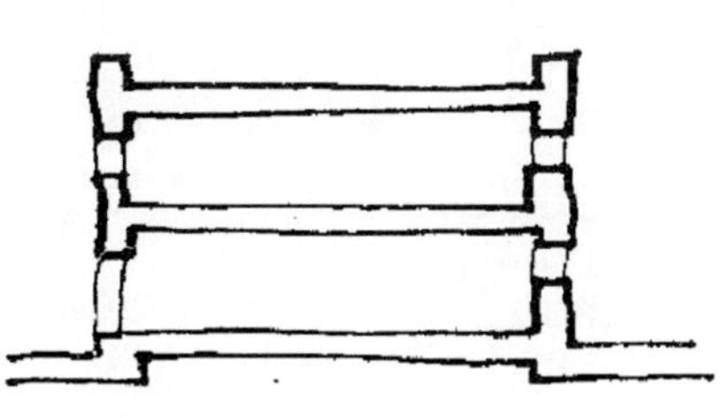

Height of each storey < 3.2 M

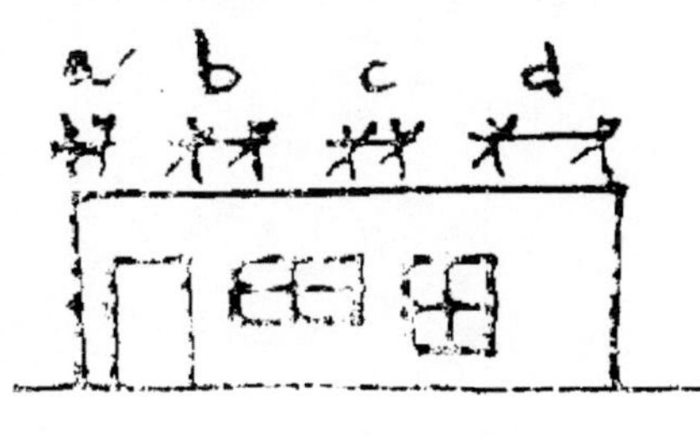

a, b, c, d < 0.6 M

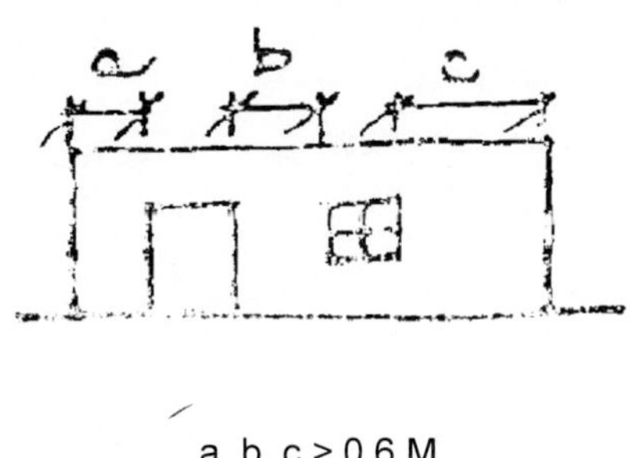

a, b, c > 0.6 M

DON'TS	**DOS**
 Foundation on rocky base.	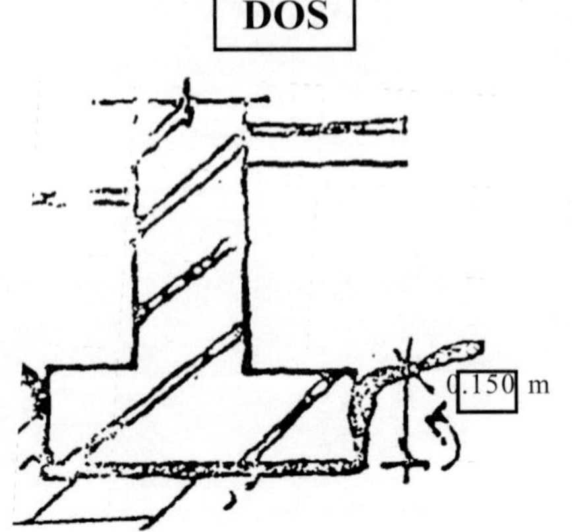 Foundation at least 0.150m inside rocky base.
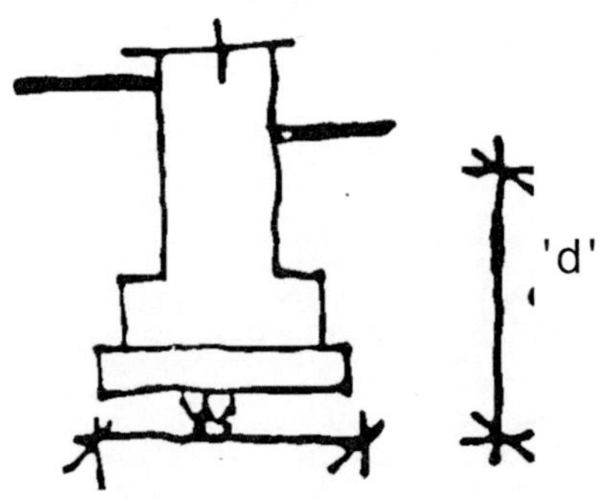 Sandy/Moorum Soil d< 0.5m W< 0.75m	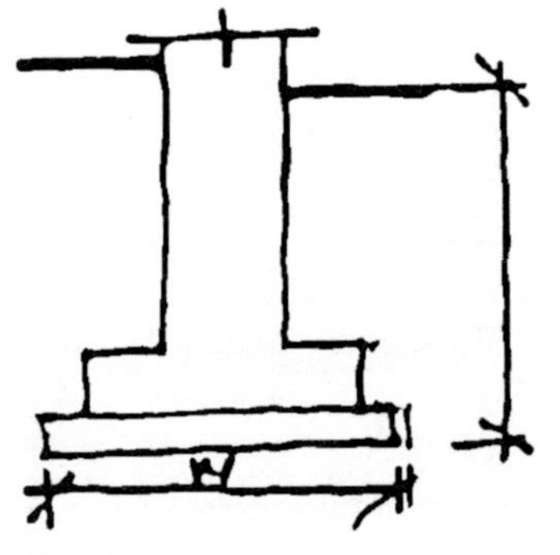 Sandy/Moorum Soil d> 0.5m W> 0.75 m
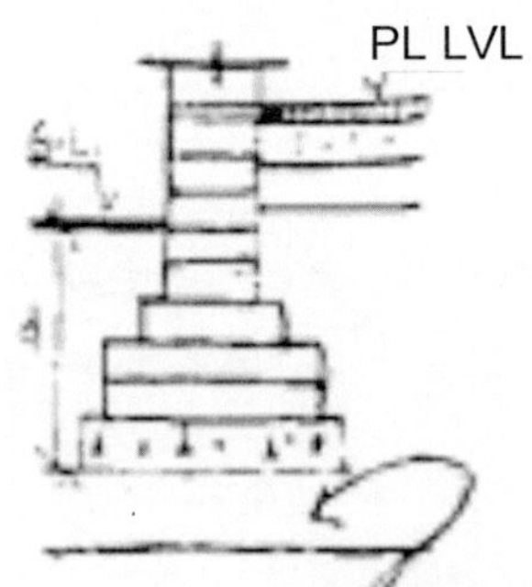 Foundation Resting on black soil where depth of soil less than 1.2 m	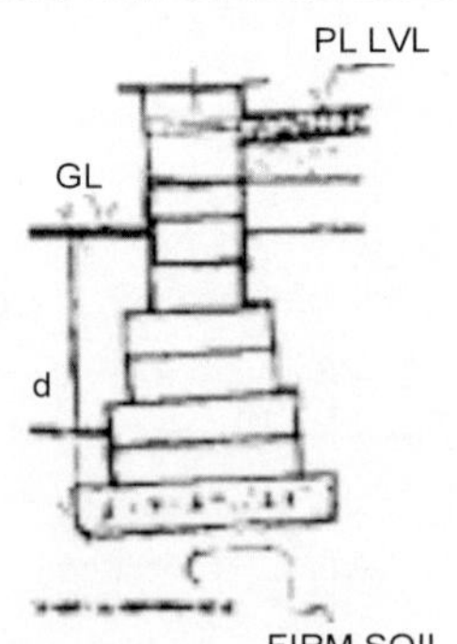 Foundation depth to be more than 1.2 m if black soil depth is 1.2 m or less.

DON'TS	DOS
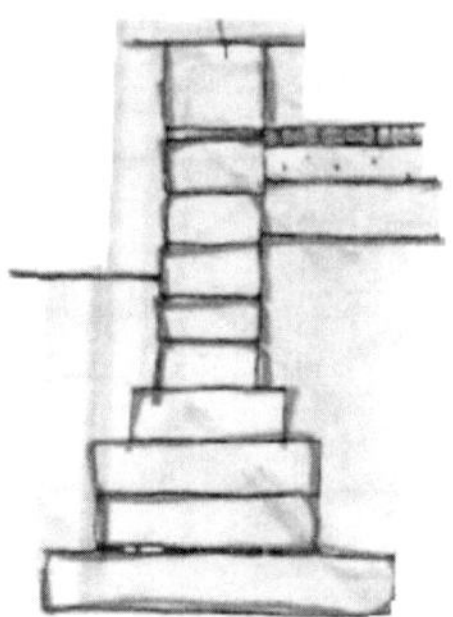 Avoid normal foundation where depth of black soil is between 1.2 m and 2.m.	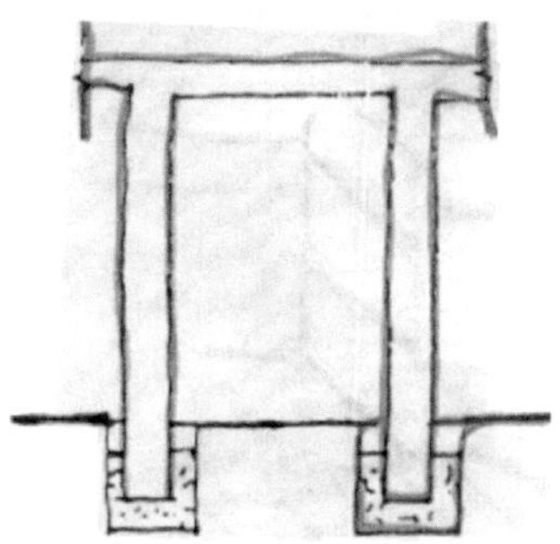 Use pedestal piles where depth of black soils is between 1.2 m and 2 m
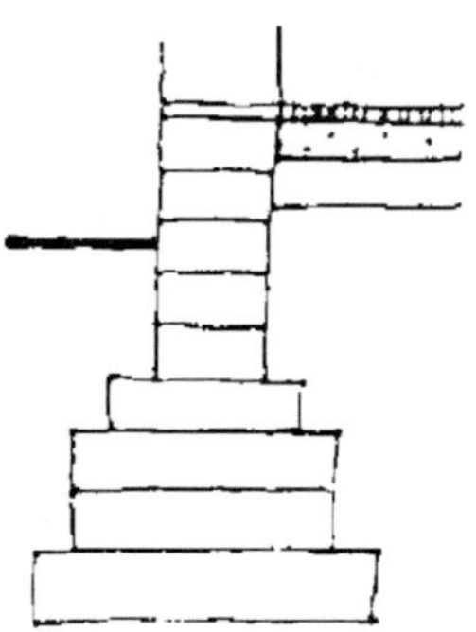 Avoid normal or pedestal foundations wherever depth of black soil is more than 2.0 m.	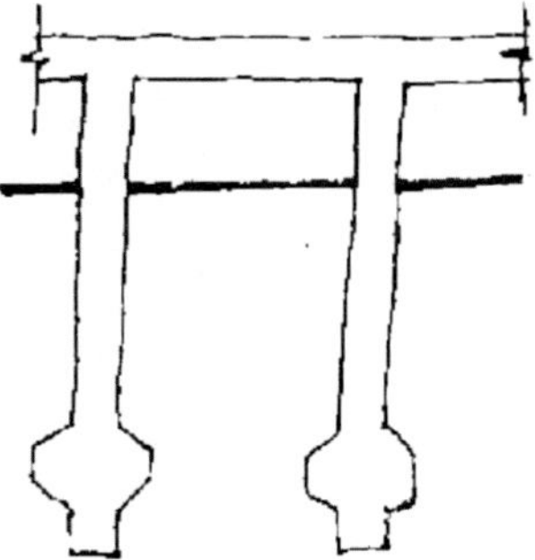 Use undereamed piles wherever depth of back soil is more than 2.0 m.
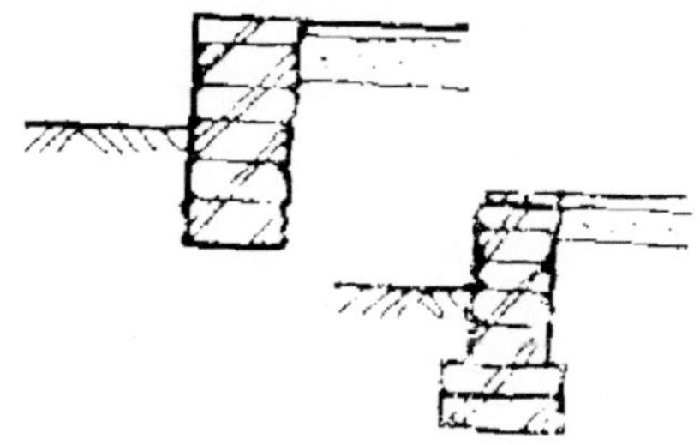 Never make a wall without a foundation. Do not use unbaked bricks or coarse sand in the foundation.	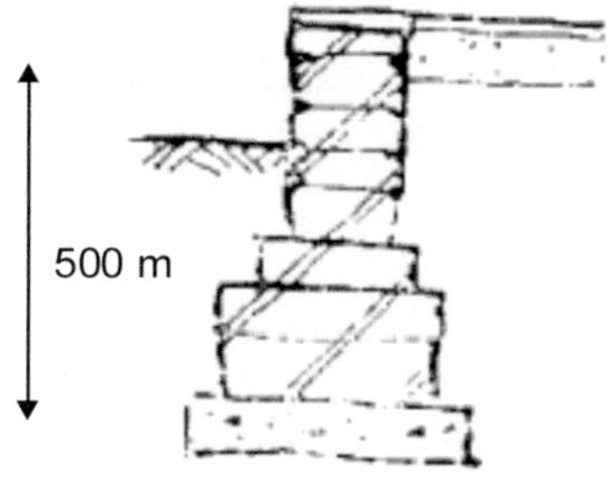 If possible, use baked bricks and stones in the foundation. The minimum depth should be 500 m.

DON'TS	DOS
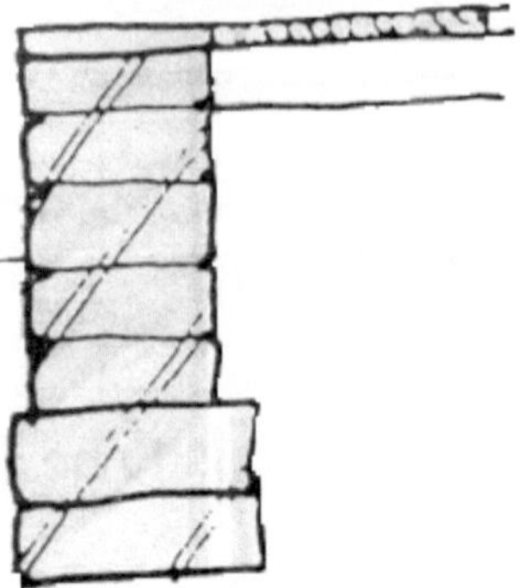	
The foundation width should not be less than one and a half times the thickness of the wall.	The foundation width should be at least one and a half times the thickness of the wall.

Walls

DON'TS	DOS
X> 6.0 M. 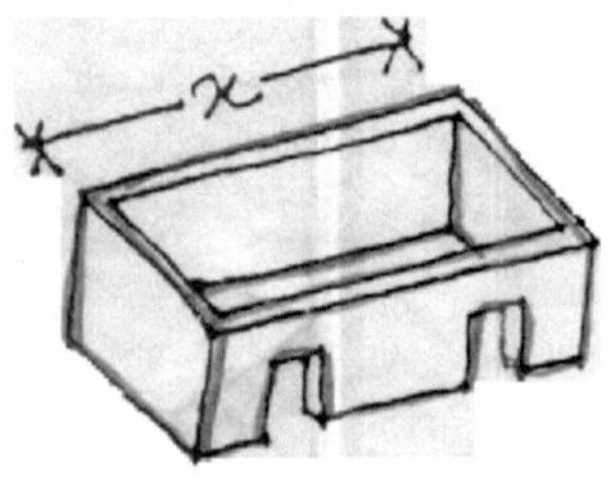	 X> 6.0 M Use cross walls of pilasters. 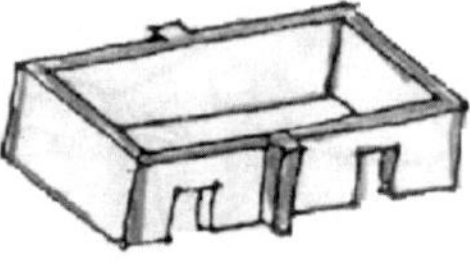
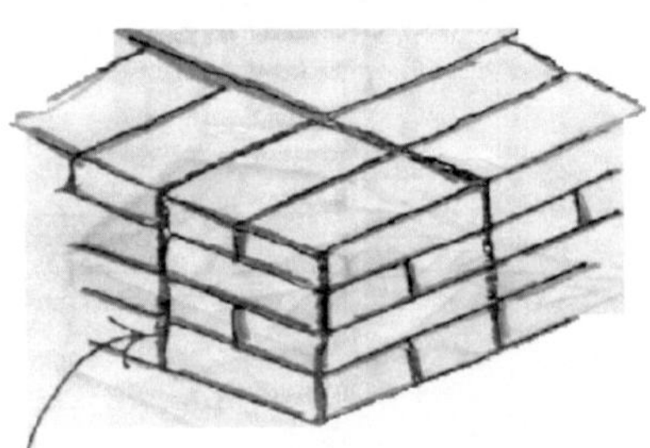 Continuation of vertical joints in courses	 Always discontinue vertical joints in each Course

DON'TS

Earthquake resistant feature for a house in a earthquake prone zone not to be without 1,2,3,4,5,6,7

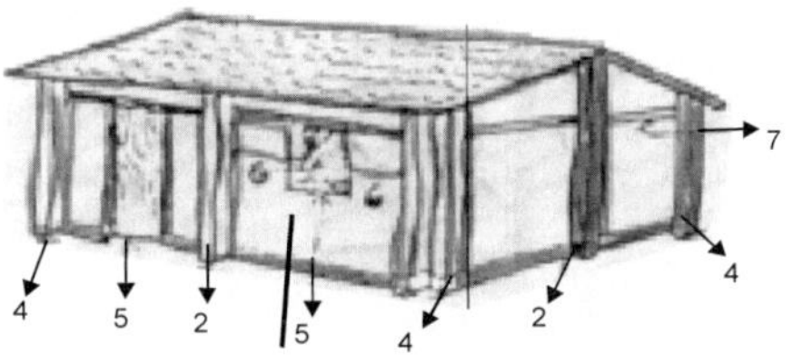

DOS

1. Wall length to be less than 10 times the thickness.
2. Buttresses between longer walls.
3. Height to be 8 times the thickness of walls.
4. Provide corner buttresses
5. Door/window openings to be kept small.
6. Distance between doors/ windows and from end of walls to doors and windows to be minimum 1200 mm.
7. Seismic band.

ROOFS

Each storey without lintel Band.

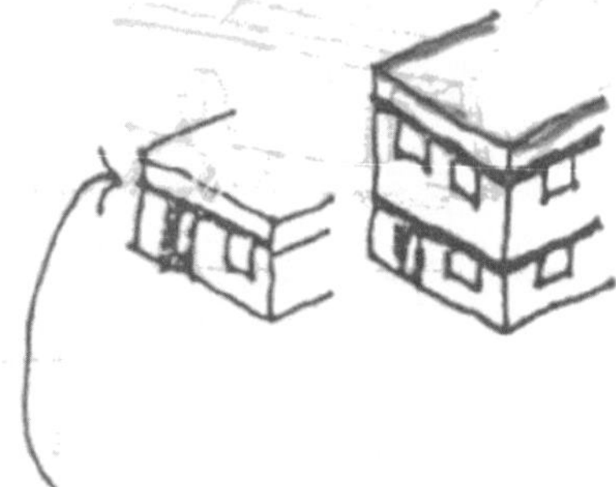

Each storey with lintel Band.

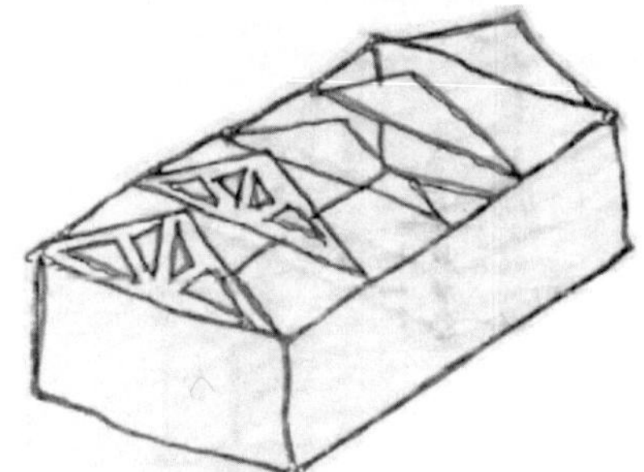

Trusses without bracings in sloped roofs

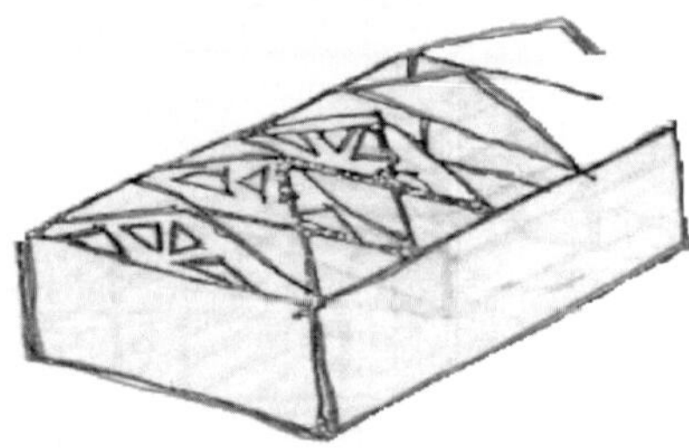

Use bracings at bottom chord and in plane of slope of trusses.

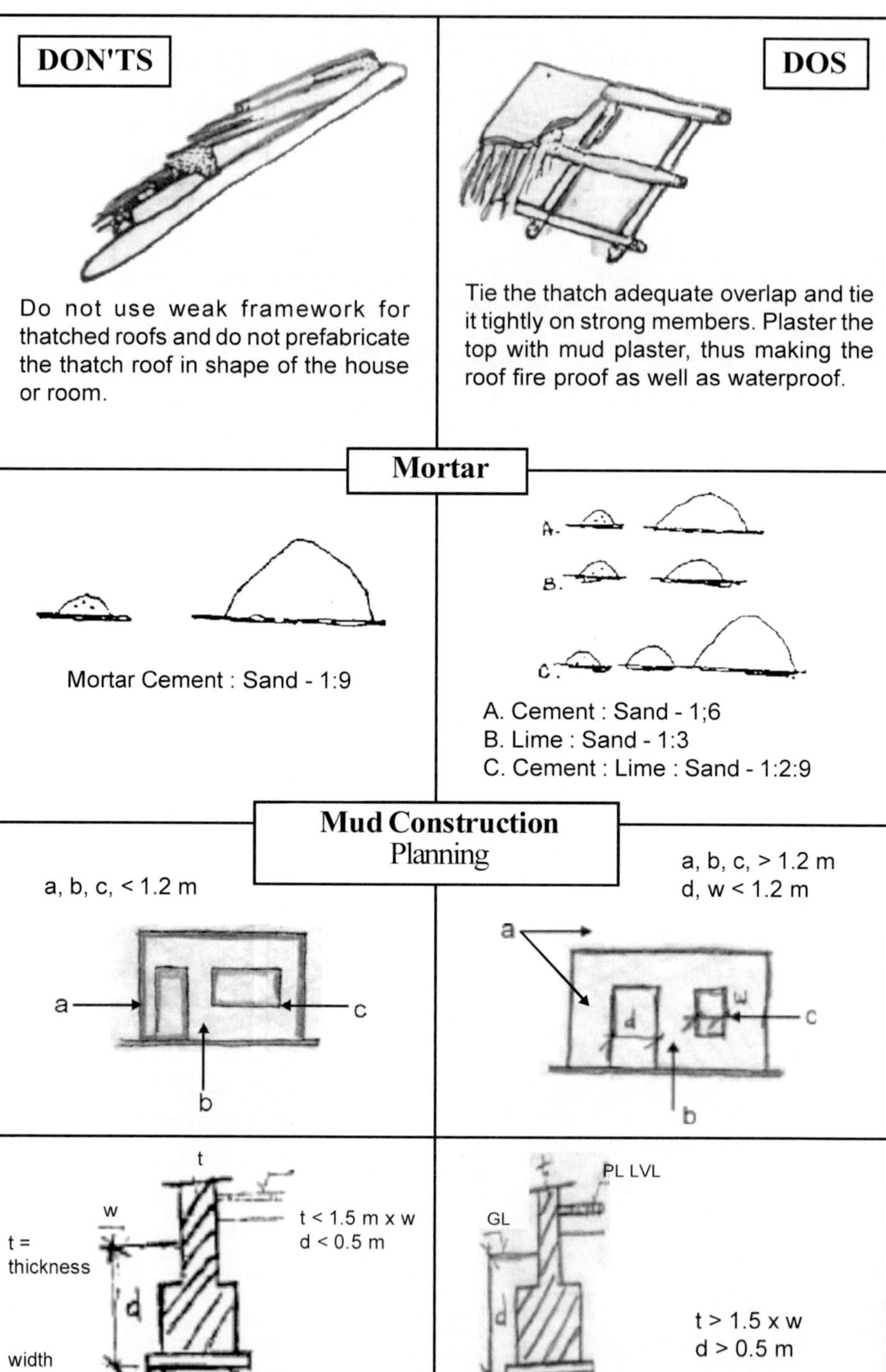
DON'TS
Do not use weak framework for thatched roofs and do not prefabricate the thatch roof in shape of the house or room.
DOS
Tie the thatch adequate overlap and tie it tightly on strong members. Plaster the top with mud plaster, thus making the roof fire proof as well as waterproof.
Mortar
Mortar Cement : Sand - 1:9
A.
B.
C.
A. Cement : Sand - 1;6
B. Lime : Sand - 1:3
C. Cement : Lime : Sand - 1:2:9
Mud Construction
Planning
a, b, c, < 1.2 m
a
b
c
a, b, c, > 1.2 m
d, w < 1.2 m
a
d
w
c
b
t
w
t = thickness
d
width
w
t < 1.5 m x w
d < 0.5 m
PL LVL
GL
d
t > 1.5 x w
d > 0.5 m

DON'TS	DOS
 Do not plaster the outer surface of an external wall with plain mud plaster.	 Plaster the outer surface with water proof mud plaster mixed with 2% bitumen cutback.
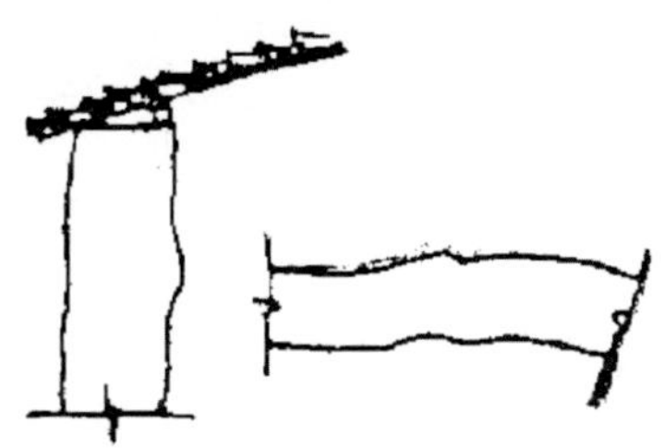 Crooked / misaligned walls in length / height.	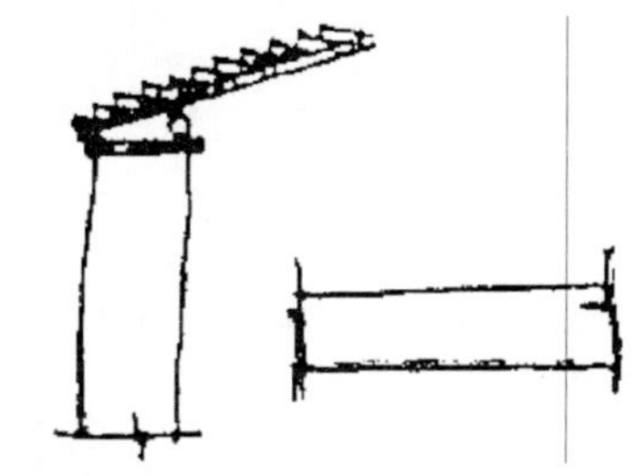 Maintain thickness of wall. Use a stone slab/wood plank over the wall.
L > 10 X W H > 8 X W 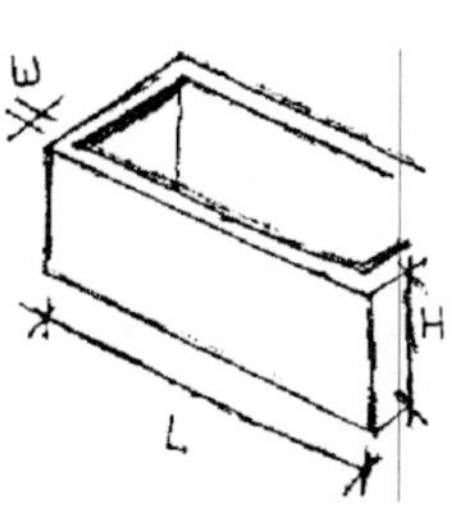	L < 10 X W H < 8 X W 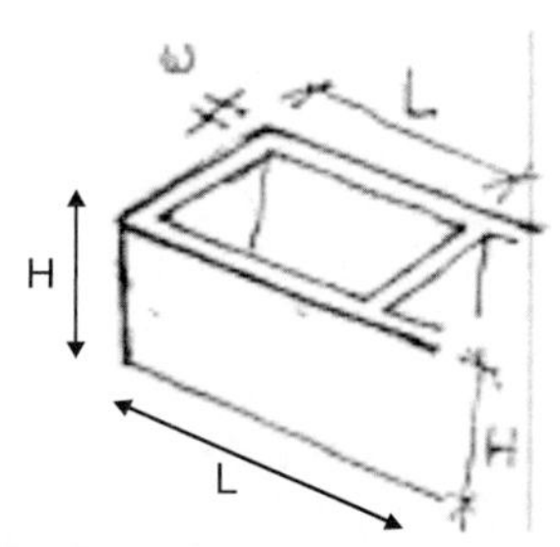
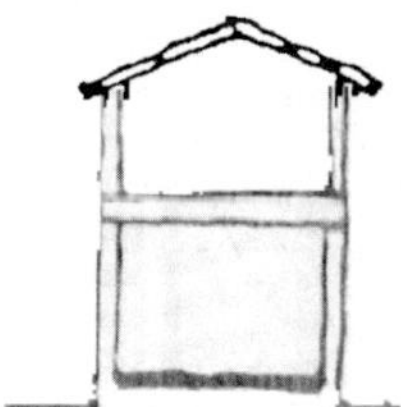 House more than 1½ storey high. Ground floor walls less than 0.35 m thick.	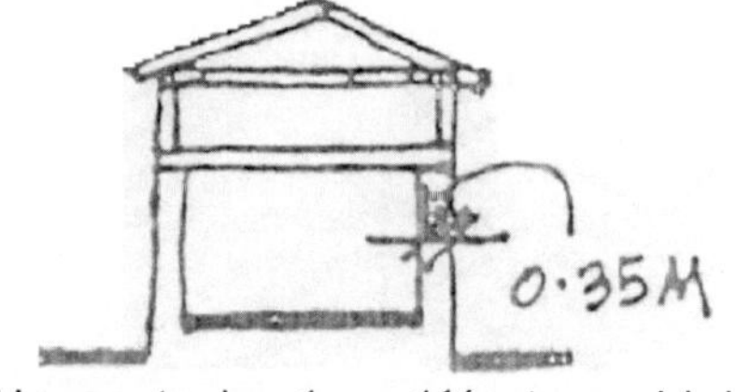 House to be 1 or 1½ storey high. Ground floor walls at least 0.35 m thick.

DON'TS	
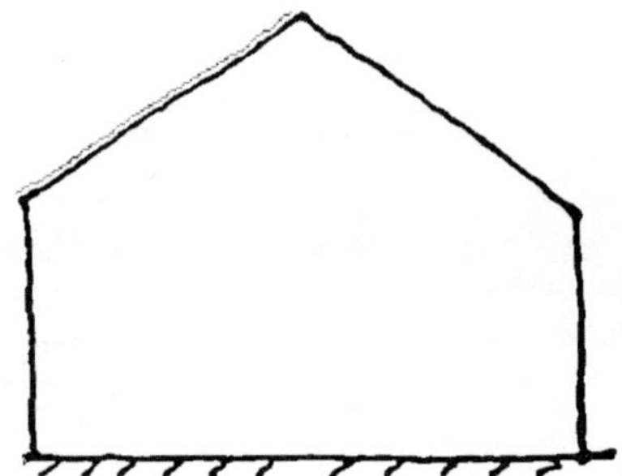 Gable wall without gable band	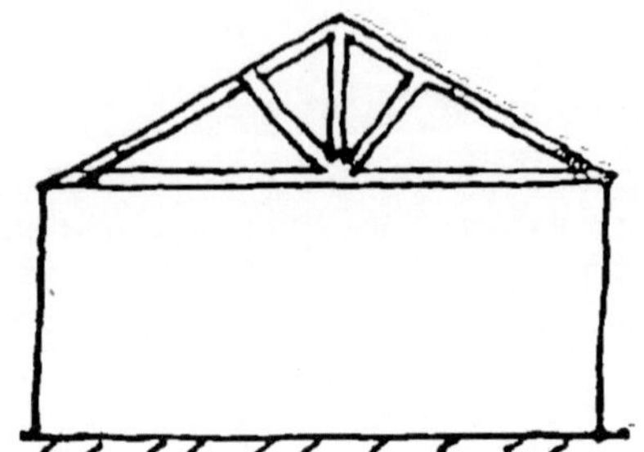 Gable wall with gable band
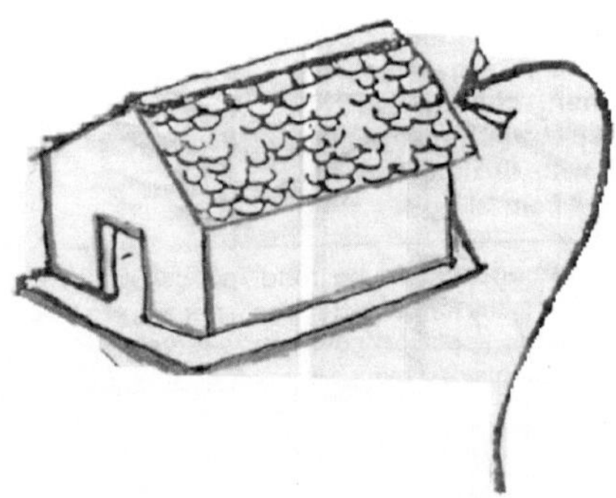 Heavy and loose elements on the roof	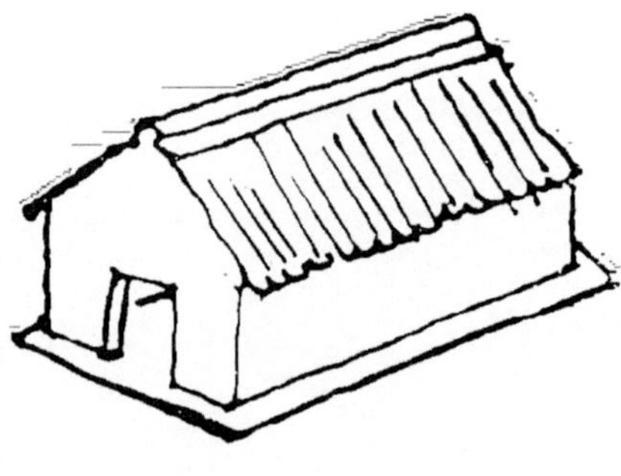 Light wt. material like sheets as roofing material Tie all elements together and with wall suitably.

DON'TS	DOS
 Engineered Buildings RCC Buildings : The columns and walls are continuous from floor to roof.	Grids of columns and beams should be laid out at right angles to each other. A good rule is that beam spans should be not less than 3m or more than 7 m.
All the centre lines of columns and beams meet each other. Columns and beams are nearly the same width. No principal members have sudden changes in cross-section. The position and area of openings should not vary significantly from floor to floor.	Columns should be uniformly distributed in plan, each carrying approximately the same amount of load. A good rule is that the area of floor carried by one column should not be more than 40 square rnetres. 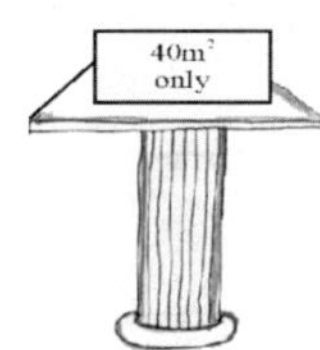
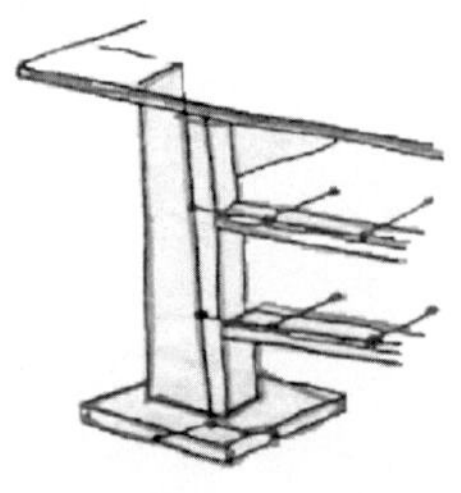 Columns and walls should be in straight lines in both directions.	Infill walls should be arranged as uniformly as possible on every floor. Wherever infill panel is structurally separated from the frame, to allow relative movement during earthquakes. It should be tied to the frame with flexible ties to prevent it from falling out. 
Congestion of reinforcement may be reduced by providing larger members. 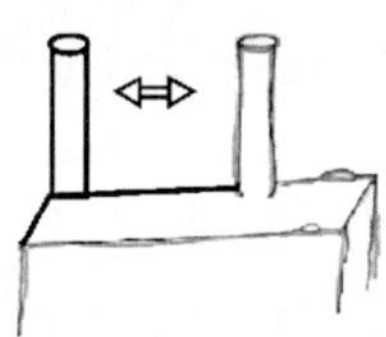 Keep spacing between bars larger than the maximum size of aggregate.	Reinforcement should be held in position in relationship to the formwork (by ties, spacers, *etc.*) and minimum specified cover to reinforcement should be maintained everywhere by non-corrding spacers 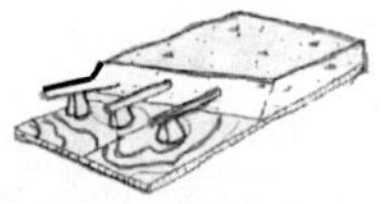

Case Study

Bhuj Earthquake : 26th January, 2001

Introduction

India due to its geological location is susceptible to most kinds of disasters 58.6% of the landmass of India is prone to earthquakes. The whole of sub Himalayan region, all the North Eastern States, the Gujarat State and Andaman and Nicobar Islands fall in IV & V seismic-zones. Earthquakes have been occuring in these areas at regular intervals. Earthquakes have taken place in Latur. Jabalpur, Chamoli, Uttarkashi, Bhuj and J&K earthquakes in the last 17 years.

Bhuj Earthquake

At about 0846 hours on 26 January 2001, when whole of India was participating in 52nd Republic Day celebrations, an earthquake of the magnitude of 6.9 on the richter scale rocked Bhuj District of Gujarat State with its epicentre east of Bhuj and close to Bhachau. It caused unprecedented and extensive damage in concentric circles in 7633 villages and 21 districts, out of 18356 villages in then 25 districts of Gujarat State. A number of towns and urban centres like Bhuj, Bhachau, Anjar, Rapar, stretching right upto Gandhinagar suffered untold destruction. Even far away urban areas like Ahmedabad, Morbi and Wankaner (district Rajkot) suffered cracks all over and buildings collapsed like nine pins. Tremors were felt in distant places like Mumbai and even Dharamshala (Himachal Pradesh). The offical figure was 13881 (unofficial more than 20,000) killed and 1.67 lac (over 3 lac unofficial) injured. Over a million houses partially or fully collapsed. In all, major social and infrastructural sectors, such as power, water supply, dams and reservoirs, schools and hospitals, the scale of destruction was truely of apocalyptic proportion.

Countless people were trapped inside the buildings, particularly in narrow lanes where many roof tops were almost touching each other. Many people tried jumping out of crashing buildings and lost limbs in the process. Initially there was shortage of wood needed for cremation in Bhuj and there was the ghory sight of dead bodies piled one over the other. The community was the first responder for quick disposal of dead bodies to avoid epidemic. Identifying the dead so that right disposal of bodies could take place as per religious customs, was a problem, faced by the police & the community.

As 26th January was a holiday, it took administration sometime to mobilize its employees from their houses for immediate deployment on search and rescue work. There were no organised and trained search and rescue teams available.

The Collector's Office in Bhuj collapsed and the Collector was made to function from under a tree. A large number of officials and their families were themselves affected and it took sometime for them to manage their families first and then report for duty, to help others.

The only satellite telephone with Bhuj Collector was non functional. The enormity of the earthquake could not be conveyed immediately to concerned higher authorities for quicker response. The entire communiction system had failed. The anxious relations and friends choked the telephone lines when telephone system was restored. The rumours were afloat as official machinery was ignorant of the magnitude of the calamity.

The Air Force was pressed into service, but Air Force Station Bhuj itself had suffered 96 deaths. The small and medium industries suffered considerable damage with large industry escaping with lesser damage due to mitigation measures taken. The migrant workers exodus created problem as they took whatever mode of transport was available to them. Kandla port suffered damages to 5 out of 10 jetties and complete collapse of telecommunication system. The situation in Navlakhi and Okha ports was worse.

Collapsed Structures in Bhuj

Response

The response from national and interntional agencies was quick. 250 international flights landed at the small airport of Bhuj. The relief material got cluttered and clogged, due to lack of space and advance planning. It took administration sometime to organise relief measures and channalise the mmediate relief. The local administration faced problems as the trucks with drivers had vanished overnight. They were victims themselves and were busy taking their families to safety. Many feared requisitioning by local authorities, without adequate compensation.

Government of India

Union Cabinet under Prime Minister and National Crises Management Committee (NCMC) under Chairmenship of Cabinet Secretary met on 26 January itself. A central team of the then experts in damage assessment was rushed to assess the situation. A Control Room was setup in Agriculture Ministry. An Empowered Group of Ministers under the Home Minister along with NCMC started functioning to monitor the situation round this clock. The Central Govt. deployed 48 AN12 & IL76 planes, 23,500 Army personnel and 3000 strong para military forces for search and rescue operations. Navy made available three ships, two of which were converted into hospitals. Teams of doctors were rushed to Bhuj. Severely injured were flown to Mumbai & other medical centres in India. Civil Avlation Ministry arranged free transportation of relief material from within the country and from abroad. Satellite phones, hot lines, HAM radios and mobile phones were pressed into service and by 2nd February 2001, all 147 telephone exchanges were restored. Railways restored the damaged tracks in both broad and metre gauge tracks by the same time.

The Deptt. of Food and Public Distribution allocated one lac tons of foodgrains and released in advance 10,000 tons of levy sugar, besides adequate quantities of diesel and kerosene. The Ministry of Power arranged for 19 large generator sets for Gujarat State Electricity Board (GSEB) at Bhuj/Anjar. The Power Grid Corporation/NTPC assisted in repairing and recommissioning 10 GEB major sub stations. Power Finance Corporation sanctioned a loan of 100 crore for repair and reconstruction of transmission and distribution system.

Immediate assistance of Rs. 500 crore was released by the Government of India from National Calamity Contingency Fund on 30 January 2001 and Rs. 330 crore was provided subsequently. Rs. 10 crore was released from PMs Relief Fund. Ministry of Rural Development made another allocation of Rs. 150 crore for reconstruction for below poverty line families. Rs. 40,000 per dwelling unit was proposed for the affected districts.

Government of Gujarat

The State Government mounted massive rescue and relief work in conjunction with Armed and para military forces. It involved 1152 JCBs/Cranes, 543 bulldozers, 2853 dumpers and trucks and 901 gas cutters. About 2100 technical personnel, 6200 non technical personnel and 13,000 labourers were mobilized. Over 763 specialist doctors, 1834 medical officers and more than 2500 para medical staff were deployed for emergency medical response.

The NGOs played a pivotal role in all phases *viz* search and rescue, relief and reconstruction of the disaster. Food was provided to individuals and community kitchens were manned by volunteers and NGOs and coordinated by State Govt officials. Nearly 21000 MT of foodgrains and about 4500 kilo litres of kerosene were supplied to Kutch alone. As the affected population had lost its purchasing power, the Government also provided each family a free kit containing 50 kg of wheat flour, 3 kg rice, one litre edible oil, potatoes, onions and spices. Nearly 600,000 blankets and over 250,000 tents and other temporary shelter material were also provided.

Cash assistance was provided to affected families at the rate of Rs. 15 per person, limited to Rs. 250 per family per month and Rs. 1250 per family for household kits to supplement their needs. In addition Rs. 1 lac per deceased person to next of kin was sanctioned. Another Rs. 50,000 was given to those children, teachers and Government employees who had taken part in Republic Day parade and died. Compensation was also paid to injured on a graded scale, subject to maximum of Rs. 50,000.

Over 6.7 lac persons were treated for various types of injuries. 20,717 persons who had sustained orthopedic, head and other serious injuries were admitted in various hospitals, nearer their homes for treatment.

Relief Camp after the earthquake

Senior state officers were rushed from Gandhinagar and other districts, to worst affected villages to coordinate relief and rescue operations, removal of debris, removing bodies trapped thereunder, arranging immediate medical assistance, restoring civic services and meeting food, shelter and other needs of workers. State Govt appointed additional collectors and additional DDOs in all 17 worst affected talukas. At the apex level, a Gujarat State Disastor Management Authority (GSDMA) headed by the Chief Minister was set up in February 2001 and a Senior Principal Secretary level officer was appointed as its Chief Executive Officer (CEO).

Based on the various announcements by the State Government a requirement of Rs. 200 crore for death relief, Rs. 142.36 crore for injured, Rs. 168.95 crore for cash doles and gratitution relief of Rs. 138.13 crore to the affected people for household kits was worked out. The total relief given in initial stages was Rs. 650 crores.

International Community

Although Government of India never formally issued an appeal for international assistance, the international community wholeheartedly responded with promptness and generosity. The Office for the Coordination of Humanitarian Affairs (OCHA) sent a five member team, which alongwith staff from United Nations Development Program (UNDP) Emergency Response Division was deployed immediately to coordinate the UN response. An Onsite

Operations Coordination Centre (OSOCC) was set up in Bhuj Collectors office compound. The OSOCC included a World Health Organisation (WHO) Disease Surveillance Desk to monitor outbreak of diseases. World Food Program gave Rs. 19 crore for food relief to 300,000 people for four months. A number of countries sent pledged cash or in kind contribution on a bilateral basis through an NGO or the UN systems. International Federation of Red Cross issued appeal for more than Rs. 70 crore to address the immediate need of affected community. Relief & Rescue Teams came from Britain, Turkey, Germany, Russia, France & Israel. UNICEF was a major player which provided major countribution towards restoring socio-infrastructure of health, nutrition, education, water and sanitation. Schools were restarted in temporary shelters, mobilizing teachers and community to ensure that there was no loss of academic year. 7830 tents were supplied to over 2000 schools. 700/800 classrooms were built by UNICEF on semi-permanent basis.

A number of countries sent fully self supporting search and rescue teams and rendered yeomans service, particularly by Swiss and Israel rescue teams, which had the most sophisticated equipment, including detection of a person whispering under piles of concrete and medical teams who could do surgical operations in the field hospitals. All teams were self contained even upto their own water requirement.

Role of NGOs

The entire nation rose as one man and came to the rescue of Gujarat in all possible ways and by all possible means. Gujarat itself is known for its spirit of mutual cooperation and self help and has a strong NGO network which quickly rallied for supporting community efforts and providing succour to the affected people. NGOs like Ramakrishna Mission, Sewa Bharati, Mata Amritanandamayi Math, Akshar Purshotam Swaminaryan Sanstha, Kutch Navnirman Abhiyan and Kutch Jain Samaj gave invaluable assistance particularly during early days of the disaster. Other NGOs which did commendable work included CARITUS India of Catholic Church of India, International Federation of Red Cross and Red Crescent Society The corporate sector also came forward with monetary and in kind help.

Reconstruction

A Public Private Partranship program was started to help in reconstruction, which was undertaken by GSDMA. A number of NGOs like FICCI-CARE venture, Manav Sadhana, Rashtriya Swabhiman,

Jai Prakash Industries etc. came forward for help. About 65 NGOs were active in Kutch alone who adopted 211 villages and constructed 32,297 houses at a cost of Rs. 185.80 crore.

Gujarat Earthquake Emergency Reconstruction Project (GEERP) was started by GSDMA with financial help from the World Bank, Asian Development Bank, Govt of India and other donar agencies. This program, unique in kind envisaged owner driven reconstruction program. Architects, engineers and masons were trained in construction of disaster resistant houses. This technical support was made available to the owners who were provided loan to reconstruct the houses. The houses were registered in the joint names of husband and wife. More than 10 lac houses have been constructed under this program; all houses being multi hazard resistant. The GEERP received international acclaim and is considered one of the good practices, emulated even by other countries.

Lessons Learnt

Initial Response : First 72 hours and especially first 24 hours after an earthquake are very crucial for rescue and relief work. The district, state and central search and rescue teams should be mobilised at the earlist. We now have NDRF teams who are highly trained in collapsed structure search and rescue (CSSR) and medical first response (MFR). States/UTs are being encouraged to raise and train at state/UT level also in this case, search and rescue took time to start.

National Building Codes : All buildings especially those in seismic zone III to V must follow the building codes, which have been revised in 2002. There should be no let up in their implementation. Supreme Court in its verdict on a PIL on 13 April 2009 has directed that all should buildings will be as per Natioal Building code and will have fire fighting equipment in it with trained faculty to operate them.

Reducing Risk and Vulnerability and Preparation of District Disaster Management Plans : Each district is peculiar in risks and vulnerability. Disaster Management Plans should be made for each district. These plans should be rehearsed periodically to find gaps in preparation and implementation. The plans should be multi hazard oriented. The states should also reduce the risk and vulnerability through capacity building, education, strengthening communication, legislation and linking development with prevention of disasters. National vision on disaster management recommends adoption of holistic approach with emphasic as prevention, mitigation and preparedness.

Search & Rescue (SAR) Teams : There was scarcity of sophisticated equipment for search and rescue teams. The search and rescue teams should be raised and trained at district and state levels also. The central SAR teams known as National Disaster Response Force (NDRF) have already been raised out of para military forces. India now has 144 SAR teams deployed in most vulnerable areas, for training & capacity development during non disaster time and for quick deployment during disasters. These SAR teams are self sustaining for disaster related rescue work. They can also manage CBRN disasters. 36 more teams are being raised.

Development : In order to avoid loss of lives due to earthquakes, Area Development Authorities and Town Planning Schemes have been set up to decongest the populated areas and have planned cities/town.

Relief Organisation. The relief material received from various quarters should be received at predesignated air, rail and road heads and organisations identified to distribute it to affected community. There should be transporancy in distribution of relief. The district authorities should also announce specific requirements of the community to avoid wastage and duplication.

Reconstruction. The reconstruction work should be taken to include the disaster resistant elements. Owner driven reconstructin strategy has proved beneficial for all. The occupancy rate has also been almost 100%. The local practices should be taken into consideration while planning reconstruction and retrofitting work. Reconstruction under GEERP is considered to be a good practice.

Capacity Building and General Awareness. The community is first responder in any disaster. General awareness about the vulnerability of the area to various disasters and actions to be taken before, during and after the disasters should be imparted to the community under capacity building program. General awareness could be spread through short films, play lets, road shows, TV and radio clips, advertisements in papers, seminars, programs, training capsules, etc.

Networking. The NGOs, Armed Forces, Para Military Forces, other stake holders like police, irrigation, electricity, water, sewerage *etc.* personnel should network together with local administration to prepare for any disaster. Mock drills should be carried out together to find gaps in preparedness.

Case Study

Eyjafjallajokull (Iceland) Volcano -2010

What is Volcanic Ash

When a volcano, charged with gases, such as sulphur dioxide and carbon dioxide erupts, it can result in large amounts of ash being generated. Now add to this, an eruption under ice and you have the added explosivity to pump the ash high into the atmosphere. Ash is made up of very fine particles of volcanic glass formed by breaking up of bubbles during the eruption. As the magma gets close to the surface the gases expand forming a volcanic froth, which then fragments into thousands of particles of ash. In the case of Iceland eruption (case study), we had added water coming into the system from the ice which flashed to steam under the heat and caused more explosions.

How does Ash affect Flying

If the volcano is powerful as with Eyjafjallajokull, it can eject the ash high in the sky into high atmospheric winds which can then blow the ash around the globe. These high winds are where our planes fly, so when volcanic eruption results in ash clouds we have to be careful not to fly through them. In the past, when planes have accidently flown through an ash cloud, the engines have clogged up with ash causing engine failure. The jet engine can have temperature upto 2000 degrees centrigrade, which will re-melt the ash back to lava and stick to the engine parts. In extreme examples, planes have had to literally glide their way out of the ash cloud before engine could be restarted. Avalanche is considered a local disaster, with earth heat and power, with lava flows, fountains and explosions but they can also influence our lives, even if we live a long way away. The whole world virtually came to standstill with the Iceland volcano.

Volcanic system is a complicated one. Like the plumbing in a bath room, it can be interconnected underground by a series of pipes and fractures. In some cases when one volcano erupts, it stirs others nearby, which may be more dangerous. In this case the neighbouring volcano, a more dangerous one, Katla, however did not get affected, for a change!!

Background

Iceland lies on the mid Atlantic Ridge, the highly volatile boundary between Euroasian and North American Continental plates, with frequent quakes and eruptions. Eyjafjallajokull Glacier is located North of Skogar and West of a larger glacier known as Myrdalsjpkull and is 120 km Southeast of the capital of Iceland, Reykjavik. This is one of the smaller glacier of the country and has been a popular hiking ground. The glacier is located on top of the volcano and is about 200 metres thick - thinner than many glaciers atop other volcanos that have erupted in recent times. That means there is less ice and water, to suffocate the eruptions and resulting steam. The volcano under the Eyjafjallajokull glacier is 5466 ft high and is ice capped by the glacier. The glacier had erupted earlier in the year 920, 1612 and continuously for over a year from end 1821 to early 1823, which had caused a fatal glacial lake outburst floods. Previous eruptions had been followed by eruptions of its larger neighbour Katla.

The Eruptions

The volcano remained dormant since 1823. At the end of Dec 2009, however, seismic activity began around the Eyjafjallajokull volcano area, with thousands of small earthquakes (mostly measuring 1-2.4 on the Richter scale, 7-10 km beneath the volcano) by 26 Feb 2010. The seismic activity led to first volcanic eruption on 20 March 2010, placing the Volcanic Explosivity Index at 1. Thereafter, regular eruptions were observed in the area. On 11 April, 2010, powerful tremors shook the countryside as eruption from the volcano hurled a steady stream of ash into the sky. Late on 13th April 2010, a new vent under the central crater opened and began spewing plume of ash (as per Nordic Volcanological Centre in Reykjavik, Iceland). The volcano generated huge amount of ash, creating voluminous ash, which in this case rose as high as 11 km. Two factors contributed to high volume of fine ash. One is the composition of the lava. The more viscous the lava is, the harder it is for the gases within it to bubble out. This tends to make it explosive throwing ash into the air. Eyjafjallajokull lava by Icelandic standards was quite viscous. The other factor is presence of water. Direct contact of molten lava with water or ice can also lead to explosion with eject fine dust. A small ice cap on top of this volcano promoted such shenanigans.

These sort of eruptions (volcano under a glacier) generate a lot of steam and volcanic gases, a lot of very fine fragments, rocks and solidified lava. Once the glacial ice around the volcano melts, the amount of ash emitted in the air gets reduced. The ash clouds also dissipate after the eruption ceases. The plume of ash chokes the upper atmosphere, where international flights generally operate.

The ash clouds, after eruption and rising to high altitude, in this case drifted southeast towards the Europe continent, sparing the capital Reykjavik and other more populated centers but forcing farmers and livestock to move indoors. As per the nearby residents, the ash was between black and grey in color and very fine similar to flour or sugar grains. Ash fell on ground unevenly and sporadically. In some places, it was up to 3mm thick.

Initially, there were fears that volcano could cause flooding, as it causes ice to melt in the glacier around it, and more than 600 people were evacuated too temporarily, but this scenario (flooding) was avoided due to less ice cover over the volcano.

While some ash fell on mostly uninhabited areas in Iceland, most was carried by westerly winds towards Europe. The volcano ash carried fine particles, which can travel longer than the heavier particles. Smoke and ash from the eruptions reduced visibility for visual navigation and microscopic debris in the ash could sandblast windscreens and melt in the aircraft turbine engines, causing engines to be damaged and to shut down. Volcanic ash can cause jet engines to fail in flight. An engine's heat melts the fine ground rocks, which proceed to encrust the cooler parts of the mechanism, stopping it from working. Lower concentration can damage engines without having an immediate effect on how well they work. But where the boundaries between danger, potential damage and safety lie and how they vary with the type and number of ash particles was not taken into account by the decision makers while deciding to close the air space. Computer models of ash clouds dispersion gave only a very broad sense of where the ash might be. This was a case of be safe than sorry later on. This is an area where the scientists would have to work and come up with a model, so that disruptions due to volcano-glacier eruptions can be minimized.

In the instant case, the plume of ash hung over most parts of Europe which led to extensive disruption of air travel from 15th April to 22nd April 2010, grounding planes and disrupting the travel plans of millions of people around the World. Airspace of more than 20 European countries remained closed for almost one week, causing as per estimate $1.7 billion financial loss to airlines. Some losses were covered by some of the European countries, but still the effect of the volcano was colossal and world-wide.

Environmental Effects and Lessons Learnt

At the mouth of the crater, the gases, ejecta and volcanic plumes created a rare weather phenomenon, known as volcanic lightning. When rocks and other ejecta collide with one another, it creates static electricity. This coupled with the abundant water & ice located at the summit, aids in creation of lightning.

High fluoride Hakla eruptions pose a threat to foraging livestocks, especially sheep. Fluoride poisoning can start in sheep at a diet of 25 ppm. At 250 ppm, death can occur within a few days. In 1793. 79% of sheep in Iceland died due to eruption in Laki volcano.

Large scale release of sulphur dioxide into the atmosphere can pose potential health risks, especially those with breathing problems, like asthma, bronchocele, pneumonia, etc.

There is a school of thought that the volcano-glacier eruption would lead to global cooling. As the glacier is one of the smaller ones, its effect, if any may be temporary, say up to a year or so. On the other hand, geologist like Andy Hooper at Delft University of Technology, has opined that mega release of CO_2 into the air is likely to add to global warming.

Another effect of the volcano eruption was, when the skies opened up after no-flying for nearly one week, the people saw the blue sky with moon and stars, after a long long time. The excessive flights (> 28000) per day, cover the skies with layers of smoke emitted from the jets.

After analysis of the satellite images, it has come to light that the volcanic ash cloud which grounded flights was so thin that it was close to undetectable. The Met Office of Britain, which is responsible for forecasting ash for Europe, uses a research plane, a BAe 146 jet, which was under repair and repainting and hence this information was not available. It has now emerged that the maximum density of the cloud was only 1/20th of the safe flying limit now in place. In absence of the research plane data, a theoretical weather model was used which predicted the cloud would cover a vast area.

Recommendations

The whole episode puts the volcanoes in a new perspective. In modern times people have become more reliant on air travel than ever before and this is likely to increase. There may be many volcanoes erupting around the world, in future. We are likely to witness further examples of volcanoes erupting ash clouds entering air space. New and innovative measures will need to be put into place to provide solution to lessons learnt from Iceland volcano eruption. Engine tests may be required, quicker new routings and even an engineering solution to make jet engines less susceptible to volcanic ash may have to be developed.

Although this phenomena (volcano and glacier eruption) is unlikely to be seen in the Indian context, eruptions elsewhere can have indirect effect on Indian air travelers getting stranded for days at various airports in the world, with some of them facing visa expiry problems.

Chapter 6

Landslides

Introduction

Landslides are simply defined as mass movement of rock, debris or earth down a slope and have come to include broad range of motions whereby falling, sliding and flowing under the influence of gravity dislodges earth material. They often take place in conjunction with earthquakes, floods and volcanoes. At times, prolonged rainfall cause heavy landslides, that block the flow of river for quite sometime.

Fig. 6.1 : How Landslides Occur

In the hilly terrain, landslides have been a major and wide spread natural disaster that often affect life and property and occupy a position of major concern. Two regions most vulnerable to landslides are Himalayas and the Western Ghats in India. As per studies carried out by Central Road Research Institute, high to very high incidence of landslides takes place in Himalayas and a high rate in the Western Ghats. Himalayas comprise of tectonically unstable younger geological formations subjected to severe seismic activity. The Western Ghats and Nilgiris in Tamil Nadu State are stable but have uplifted plateau margins influenced by neo-tectonic activity. Compared to Western Ghats, landslides in Himalayan are huge and massive and in most cases the overburden along-with the underlying lithology is displaced during sliding, particularly due to seismic factor. In contrast, the landslides in Western Ghats are confined to over burden without affecting the bedrock beneath and are generally in the nature of debris flows occurring mainly during monsoons. The effect, of course, is felt much more acutely because of a comparatively higher density of population.

Onset, Type and Warning

Though landslides occur gradually, however, sudden failure (sliding) can occur without warning. They may take place in combination with earthquakes, floods and volcanoes. There are no clearly established warnings in place indicating occurrence of landslides and hence difficult to predict the actual occurrence. Areas of high risk can be determined by use of information on geology, hydrology, vegetation cover, post occurrence and consequences in the region. Scientists have of late developed instruments which can predict onset of landslides and give adequate warning. Its commercial use has however not yet started.

Elements at Risk

The most common elements at risk are the settlements built on the steep slopes, built at the toe and those built at the mouth of the streams emerging from the mountain valley. All those buildings constructed without appropriate foundation for a given soil and in sloppy areas are also at risk. Typical example is Sanjauli area in Shimla Roads, communication line and buried utilities are other facilities which are vulnerable.

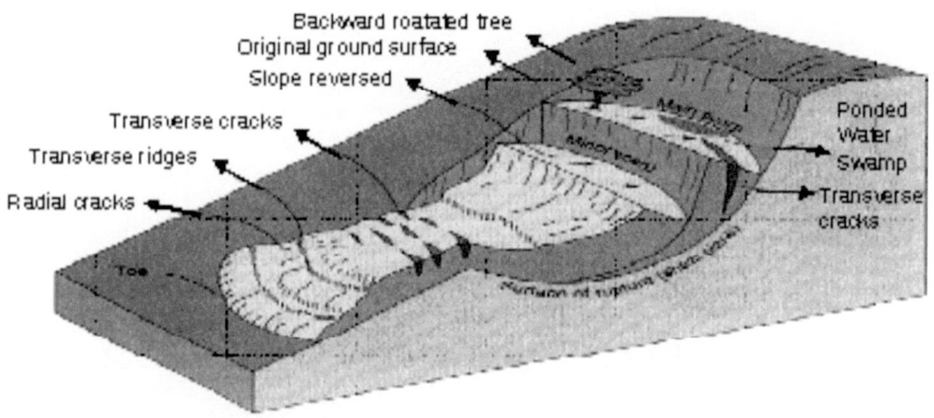

Fig. 6.2 : Diagrammatic Layout of Landslide

Effects

Landslides destroy anything that comes in their path. They block busy roads, rail lines, lines of communication, settlements, river flows, agricultural production and land area. In addition, physical effects such as flooding may also occur. They cause fatalities depending on the place and time of ocurrence.

Causes of Landslides

Landslides can be caused by poor ground conditions, geomorphic phenomena, natural physical forces and quite often due to heavy spells of rainfall, coupled with impeded drainages.

Ground Causes

- Weak, sensitivity or weathered materials.
- Adverse ground structure (joints, fissures *etc.*)
- Physical property variation (permeability, plasticity *etc.*)

Morphological Causes

- Ground uplift (volcanic, tectonic *etc.*)
- Erosion (water, wind)
- Scour
- Deposition loading in the slope crest
- Vegetation removal (due to forest fire, drought conditions, jhuming *etc.*)

Physical Causes

- Prolonged precipitation
- Rapid draw-down
- Earthquake
- Volcanic eruption
- Thawing
- Shrink and swell
- Artesian pressure

Man-made Causes

- Excavation or querrying (particularly at the toe of slope)
- Loading of slope crest
- Draw-down (of reservoir)
- Deforestation
- Irrigation
- Mining
- Artificial vibrations
- Water impoundment and leakage from utilities.

Settlement Policy

Avoid permanent settlements in high risk zones.

Site selection even in moderately safe zones, especially in plateau edge region be made with caution.

Diversion of stream channel in upper slopes, especially above settlement should be strictly disallowed.

Adequate provision for drainage of storm water away from high sloping terrain, to reduce over saturation.

Any contour bunding, or terracing adopted for seasonal cultivation or initiation of plantation in slopes of >16° above settlement should have sufficient provision for storm water drainage.

Maintain existing natural drainage channels and hallows, without any blocking, division or modification.

Mitigatory Measures

Hazard Mapping : It will locate areas prone to slope failures. This will also help in construction activities and in town and area development planning.

Proper Drainage & Drainage Correction : The most important triggering mechanism for movement is water infiltrating into overburden during heavy rains and consequent increase in pore pressure within the overburden. When this happens in steep slopes the safety factor of the slope material gets considerably reduced causing it to move down. Hence the natural way of preventing this situation is by reducing infiltration and allowing excess water to move without hindrance. As such the first step in mitigation is drainage correction. In rural and urban areas, responsibility should be borne by local self government, the community and the family.

Engineered structures with strong foundations can with stand or take the ground movement forces. Underground installations (pipes, cables etc.) should be made flexible to move in order to withstand forces, caused by the landslides.

Insurance : It will assist individuals whose homes are likely to be damaged by landslides. For new constructions it (insurance) should be made complusory.

Community Based Mitigation : Communities can play a vital role in identifying the areas where there is laid instability. Compacting ground locally, slope stabilization (terracing and true planting) and avoiding construction of houses in hazardous locations that communities can adhere to prevent landslides.

Proper Landuse Measures : Leave aside 'critical zones' where settlements could be avoided altogether and which could preferably be used for permanent vegetation like forest organizing ground. Existing natural vegetation to be preserved. Over population should be avoided and undeveloped colonies should be developed and not regularised.

Retaining Wall : Can be built to stop land from slipping. It is constructed to prevent smaller sized and secondary landslides that often occur along the toe portion of the large landslides.

Reforestation of the Areas Occupied by Degraded Vegetation : Ecological battalions employed by states (ex-servicemen) have done a wonderful job in Rajasthan and Uttarakhand. Similar battalions or such organizations can be raised in affected areas by the states. Increasing vegetation cover is cheapest and most effective way of arresting landslides. This helps to bind top layer of soil with layers below while preventing excessive run off and soil erosion.

Development Activities : Development activities should be taken up only after a detailed study of the region. Slope protection if necessary should be done. Avoid construction of roads, irrigation canals etc. along natural drainage. Total avoidance of settlements in risk zone is recommended.

Creation of Awareness Among Local Population : The responsibility should rest on the local administration, the community and non government organizations.

Response (Individual / Family Level)

What to do if you suspect imminent landslide danger :

- Contact your local fire and/or police control rooms.
- Inform neighbours who are likely to be affected. It would help save lives. Help them in evacuation, if required.
- Evacuation out of the likely path of the landslide is the best protection. Take your emergency kit, containing valuables, important documents, some cash and the family kit containing emergency rations, water, torch, transistor, spare batteries, 1-2 days food and first aid box.

What to do during a Landslide

- Quickly move out of path of the landslide or debris flow.
- If inside a building, stay inside and take cover under a desk, table or other sturdy furniture.
- If escape is not possible, curl into a tight ball and protect your head.

What to do after a Landslide

- Check for injured and trapped persons, without entering the slide. Mark likely or identified places where persons are trapped, with flags and lights. Direct rescuers to their locations.
- Help vulnerable group persons in neighbourhood for emergency assistance.

- Listen to local radio or television station.
- Watch for flooding, which may occur after a landslide or debris flow.
- Look for and report damaged utility lines to authorities.
- Check building foundation, chimney and surrounding land for damage.
- Replant damaged ground as soon as possible since erosion caused can lead to flash flooding.

Seek professional advice for evaluation of landslide hazard or designing corrective techniques to reduce landslide risk.

Highlights of Important Recommendations in NDMA Guidelines on Landslides

Although management of landslides requires coordinated and multifaceted activities among many stake-holders in the total DM cycle, a few important recommendations made are listed below :

- Developing and continuously updating the inventory of landslide incidences affecting the country.
- Landslide hazard zonation mapping in macro and meso scales after identification and prioritization of the areas in consultation with Border Road Organisation, State Governments and local communities.
- Taking up pilot projects in different regions of the country with a view to carryout detailed studies and monitoring of selected landslides to assess their stability status and estimate risk.
- Setting pace setter examples far stabilization of slides and also setting up early warning systems depending on the risk evaluation and cost benefit ratio.
- Complete site specific studies of major landslides and plan treatment measures and encourage state governments to continue these measures.
- Setting up institutional mechanisms far generating awareness and preparedness about landslide hazard among various stakeholders.
- Enhancing landslide education, training of professionals and capacity development of organisations working in the field of landslide management.

- Capacity development and training to make the response regime more effective
- Development of new codes and guidelines on landslide studies and revision of existing ones.
- Establishment of an autonomous national centre for landslide research studies and management.

Conclusion

Landslides are common phenomenon in mountains. Landslide areas are generally known. These should not be used for habitation. If one is alert he/she can avoid getting injured, by evacuating from landslide area, before land.

Chapter 7

Cyclones

Introduction

The World Meteorological Organisation (WMO) uses the term 'Tropical Cyclone' to cover weather systems in which winds exceed 'gale force' (minimum of 34 knots or 63 kmph). Tropical cyclones are the most destructive of the seasonally recurring rapid onset natural hazards. Between 80 and 100 tropical cyclones occur around the world every year. Tropical cyclones occur most in developing countries as they are the ones located close to tropical zone/s. Tropical cyclones are the progeny of ocean and atmosphere powered by the heat from the sea, driven by the easterly trades and temperate westerlies, the high planetary winds and their own fierce energy. As a combined result, the ocean develops devastating surge, inundating vast coastal areas. Due to climate changes the coastal areas, which house three billion people, (about half of population of the earth), the No. of cyclones/tornadoes/hurricanes have increased. 46 million people get affected and three million people are rendered homeless every year around the globe.

13 State / Union Terrtories consisting of 84 districts in India are vulnerable to cyclones. The East Coast is more prone to cyclones than the west coast. In the past about 2½ centuries, 21 out of 24 cyclones with heavy loss of human lives (> 10,000) in the world, look place in these areas. This was due to very serious storm surge problem in the region. Shallow bay, low flat zigzag terrain, high astronomical tide, high density of population, socioeconomic conditions, lack of awareness, inadequate prepared ness and absence of hedging mechanisms add to the problem. Every year on an average, five to six cyclones are formed in the Bay of Bengal and the Arabian sea, of which 2-3 may become severe. Incidently more cyclones are formed in Bay of Bengal than in the Arabian Sea (Fig. 7.1). Cyclones are seasonal. Severe cyclones generally occur in the months of May, June, October and November.

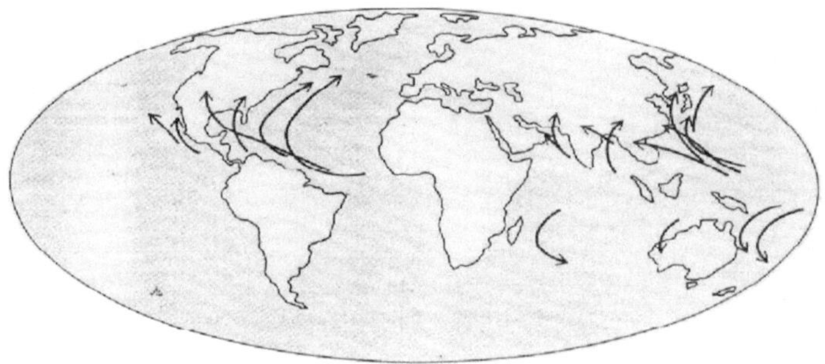

Fig. 7.1 : Cyclone routes on a world map

Characteristics

Tropical cyclones are characterized by destructive winds, storm surges and exceptional levels of rainfall, which may cause flooding :

- *Destructive Winds :* Strong winds that blow anti clockwise in Northern Hemisphere, while spiraling inwards and increasing towards the cyclone center are highly destructive. Wind speeds progressively increase towards the core as they move. As the 'eye' of cyclone arrives near landfall (winds hitting coast) winds decrease to become almost calm but rise again just as quickly as the 'eye' passes and are replaced by hurricane force winds from a direction nearly the reverse of those previously blowing.

- *Storm Surge :* It is defined as the rise in sea level above the normally predicted astronomical tide, is frequently a key or overriding factor in a tropical disaster. Major factors in its size and intensity include:
  - A fall in atmospheric pressure over the sea surface.
  - The effect of the wind.
  - The influence of the sea bed.
  - A funnelling effect.
  - The angle and speed at which the storm approaches the coast.
  - The tides.
- *Exceptional Rainfall Occurrence :* The world's highest rainfall spread over one or two days has occurred during tropical cyclones. The very high specific humidity condenses into exceptionally large raindrops and giant cumulus clouds, resulting in high precipitation rates. When a cyclone makes landfall, the rain rapidly saturates the catchment areas and the rapid runoff may extensively flood the usual water sources or create new ones.

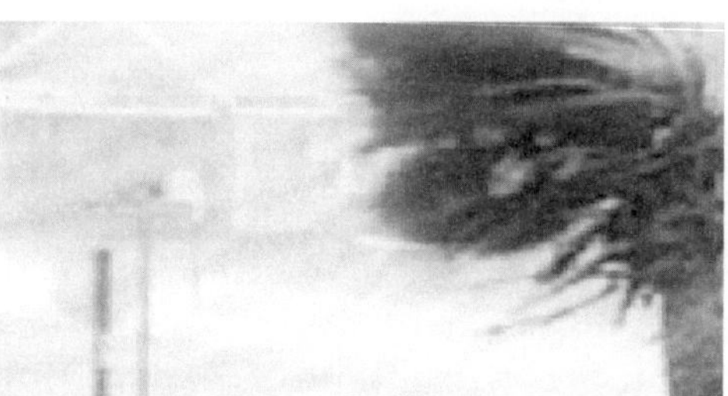

Fig. 7.2 : Strong winds during cyclone

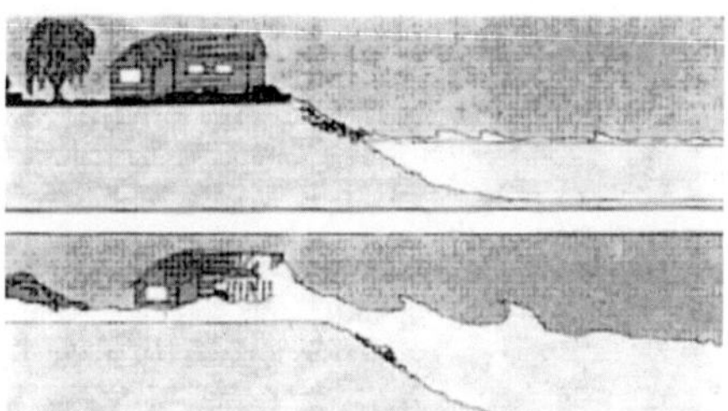

Fig. 7.3 : Strom surge in cyclone

Fig. 7.4 : Excessive rain during cyclone

Fig. 7.5 : Satellite picture of a tropical cyclone

How are Tropical Cyclones Formed

Development of cycle of tropical cyclones may be divided into three stages :

- Formation and initial development.
- Full maturity.
- Modification or decay.
- *Formation and Initial Development Stage:* Four atmospheric and oceanic conditions are necessary for development of a cyclone storm:
- A warm sea temperature in excess of 26 degrees centigrade to a depth of 60 metres, which provides abundant water vapour in the air by evaporation.
- High relative humidity of the atmosphere to a height of above 7000 metres facilitates condensation of water vapour into water droplets and clouds release heat energy thereby inducing a drop in pressure.
- Atmospheric instability encourages formation of massive vertical cumulus cloud convection with condensation or rising air over ocean.
- A location of at least 4-5 latitude degree from the equator allows the influence of the forces due to the earth's rotation to take effect in reducing cyclonic wind circulation around low pressure centers.

Mature Tropical Cyclones : The main physical feature of a mature tropical cyclone is a spiral pattern of highly turbulent giant cumulus thunder cloud bands. These bands spiral inwards and form a dense highly active central cloud core which wraps around a relatively calm and cloud free 'eye'. The 'eye' has a diameter of from 20-60 km of light winds and looks like a black hole or dot surrounded by white clouds. In contrast to the light wind conditions in the 'eye', the turbulent cloud formation extending outwards from the 'eye' accompany winds of upto 250 kilometre per hour, sufficient to destroy or severely damage most non-engineered structures in the affected communities.

Modification or Decay : A tropical cyclone begins to weaken in terms of its central low pressure, internal warm core and extremely high winds as soon as its source of warm moist air begins to ebb or are abruptly cut off. The weakening of a cyclone does not mean the danger to life and property is over. Where the cyclone hits land, especially over mountainous or hilly terrain, riverine and flash flooding may last for weeks.

Early Warning

Cyclone can be detected and predicted sometime in advance before it affects the population. A better early warning system with Doppler radar and satellite detection and monitoring can give advance warning upto 96 hours. But the area of correct landfall can be predicted upto 24 hours. Hence in effect the administration and community get approximately 18-22 hours effective warning for evacuation, provided the alarm system is in place. The losses can be minimized by organizing effective early warnings, alarm system and adequate response.

In India, India Meteorological Department (IMD) provides cyclone warnings to stakeholders through its Area Cyclone Warning Centres/ Cyclone Warning Centres and Coordination Centres located at strategic locations along the vulnerable coast line. Cyclones are tracked with the help of conventional observations, ship's reports, ocean data buoy, cyclone detection radars, Indian Geostationary Satellites (INSAT) and polar orbiting satellites. Aircraft reconaissance facilities which are one of the important tools for cyclone observations and tracking are currently not available in this region.

Warnings are communicated though various communication modes like teleprinters, telex, telephone, fax, frequent radio broadcasts, community radios, cable network, television, print media, wireless including (POLNET), para military, railway, internet and through satellite based Cyclone Warning Dissemination System (CWDS). CWDS is a unique system in India to communicate. Warnings can also be given through SMS.

Stages of Warning

The warnings to DM officials at Centre, State and district level are issued in four stages by IMD.

- Stage 1 : Cyclone Watch (72-96 hours before landfall)
- Stage 2 : Cyclone Alert (48 hours before landfall)
- Stage 3 : Cyclone Warning (24 hours before landfall)
- Stage 4 : Post landfall outlook (12 hours before landfall)

Warnings contain various information related to cyclone like its position, speed, direction of movement, anticipated adverse weather etc. Impact of cyclone on common objects on land is also included when cyclones landfall is imminent. Cyclone Warning tools and infrastructure, are being further strengthened for improved services.

Contingency Action Plan

There is a Contingency Action Plan, which spells out actions to be taken by various agencies on receipt of various cyclone threats. At the Ministry of Home Affairs (MHA), there is a 24 x 7 control room which coordinates all activities at the centre level with states when cyclone warnings are issued. Emergency Control Centre at NDMA also tracks and monitors movement of cyclones.

Alert System

Community is alerted through the various alert systems prevailing in the areas, like through broadcast from religious places, community radios, FM and local, cable network besides sirens and word of mouth and other traditional systems.

Cyclone Mitigation

NDMA has issued comprehensive guidelines for the management of cyclones in the country. These are avilable on NDMA website (www.ndma.gov.in). A comprehensive project, known as National Cyclone Risk Mitigation Project has been initiated with a view to mitigate the cyclone risk in 84 districts of 13 coastal states / UTs, in collaboration with the World Bank. Various mitigation projects like coastal afforestation, construction of cyclone shelters, raising of bunds, lateral and horizontal arteries, general awareness programmes and last mile connectivity are being taken up under this project. NDMA has also taken initiative on spreading general awareness and creating a culture of preparedness in the community through mock exercises in all vulnerable states / UTs of India.

Earliar a Disaster Risk Mitigation (DRM) program in association with UNDP in 169 most hazard prone districts (including 64 coastal districts) in the country for Capacity Building and training at grass root level was very successfuly completed by Govt. of India. National Institute of Disaster Management (NIDM) and ATIs at State level have also been building the capacity of DM officials at the Govt. and Non-Govt. Sectors.

Concept of Protecting People during Cyclones

To protect the vulnerable population from tropical cyclones, the concept adopted is to temporarily evacuate the people on receipt of warnings and look after them for 2 to 3 days by arranging shelters, food, health care facilities. Once the water levels recede and normalcy is restored, people are sent to their houses. This concept is adopted even in advanced countries like USA & Japan.

Specific Preparedness Measures

An Integrated Warning/Response System

Specific preparedness measures to counter the impact of tropical cyclones may be classified into two categories, namely long term and short term:

- *Long Term Measures :* The long term or seasonal measures need to be planned, implemented and operationally tested and co-ordinated by means of simulation exercises well before a seasonal threat commences. Among these are pre-season co-ordination meetings held at DDMA and local levels. In these meetings operational contingency plans are reviewed and amended, if need be thereafter training and community preparedness programs are conducted and community inspections made of all facilities and services that constitute community lifelines.
- *Short Term Measures :* These relate to a operationalization of SOPs, which get activated once a contemporary cyclone threat is announced. Among these are domestic, vocational and animal husbandry arrangements to safeguard the survival, property assets and livelihood of individual families and animals.

Public Warning System

The three main objectives in a tropical cyclone warning are:

- To alert the people to the danger by announcing the existence of a threat due to a cyclone.
- To identify the areas where people will be actively threatened by cyclone and where communities should monitor further warning announcements, and
- To call the people to action by recommending specific preparedness activities, which may be part of an integrated warning/response plan to protect vulnerable resources.

Training and Community Participation

Systematic methods must be employed to inform people about the threat of a disaster. There are several methods of promoting public information and education:

- Public dissemination of information through mass media like radio, television, newspapers including vernacular, poster campaigns, town councils and village meetings.
- Education programmes. Separate designs for different age levels may be offered in schools, universities and to locals as part of curriculum.
- Training programmes should be offered for local officials who will play a part in disaster mitigation, preparedness and post disaster assistance.
- Community based training that emphasies post disaster activities to be given at village and taluk level.

Post Disaster Assistance

The initial response by local authorities should (Municipality/ Taluk/Village) include:

- Evacuation of vulnerable population
- Activation of cyolone shelter
- Search and rescue for stranded people
- Medical assistance at shelters
- Provision of food and water for 24-48 hours, in shelters / safe houses
- Purification of drinking water
- Epidemiological surveillance
- Re-opening of roads
- Re-establishment of communication networks and contact with remote areas
- Debris clearance
- Damage assessment
- Coastal replantation, especially low lying and open flat areas.

Cyclone Shelters : One of the most successful means of reducing loss of human lives during cyclones, is the provision of cyclone shelters. In densely populated areas, where large scale evacuation is not usually possible, elevated community buildings, buildings used for large gatherings like schools, dharmshalas, hospitals, prayer halls, temples, churches, community halls, marriage halls etc can be used as cyclone shelters. They should be so designed as to provide a blank conical facade with minimum apertures in the direction of prevailing winds. Shorter side of building should face the storm. Alternately these buildings can be designed on a circular/ellipsoidal plan so as to impart least wind resistance. These shelters should be located in relatively elevated areas with provision for community kitchen, water supply, sanitation and first aid. Individual shelters fabricated in concrete and steel can be attached to existing dwellings. Shelter is installed 4 feet in the ground, and the mud from excavation is placed around shelter, to help increase shelters effectiveness. Elevated mounds near shellers should be made for animals. Cattles can also be accommodated in the open ground floor of the shelters. The provision should exist for ramps for easy access of shelters by disabled persons.

Do's and Don'ts before, during and after a Cyclone (For Individual)

- Check your house, repair doors and windows, wherever necessary, before April month.
- Keep a hurricane lantern filled with kerosene, flashlight, match boxes, candles and enough dry cells.
- Make sure that your radio set is fully serviceable. Keep an extra set of batteries ready for transistor.
- On receipt of warning, fill up overhead water tanks.
- Install elevated hand pumps for drawing drinking water in first/ second floor.
- Bolt up glass windows and put storm shutters in place.
- Get extra food stored, particularly the type which does not require long cooking, such as, flat rice, sattu (pulse powder) maggie, soups and long life 'chapati' (Indian breed). Precooked food by Defence Food Research Laboratory, Mysore is not only nutritious but tasty too. Store extra drinking water.

- When you are moving to a shelter, shift your articles to upper floors or tie it to the ceiling so that these would not be submerged in water.
- Don't venture into the areas where streams or rivers flow; high water due to heavy rains, may surge.
- Make provisions for children, disabled, destitutes and old people requiring special diet/help.
- Be calm. Your ability to meet an emergency will inspire and help others.
- Stay in the shelter, as long as you are informed to do so.
- While in the shelter, follow the instructions of person/s-in-charge.

Don'ts (For Community)

- Do not keep loose objects like cans, tins and other implements. They may become weapons of destruction during strong winds.
- Do not spread rumours, nor listen to them, only official version of the warnings may be listened to through radio/TV.
- Do not stay in your house if it is not safe and when advised to vacate by authorities, especially when your house is located in a low lying area. You may run the risk of being marooned.
- Do not venture out, if the weather suddenly clears during a storm as indicated by a lull in the wind and rain. Remember strong wind will return equally suddenly from the opposite direction, with even greater velocity. This happens when the 'eye' of the storm passes over your area.
- Avoid any loose wires, hanging from the poles to prevent electrocution.
- Drink only safe and purified water.

Action Points

Action before the first warning [48 hours before Cyclone Alert] Steps to be taken before the cyclone season by the community.

- Check your house, secure loose tiles by cementing wherever necessary, repair doors and windows.
- Check the area around the house, remove dead or dying trees, anchor removable objects, such as, lumber piles, loose zinc sheets, loose bricks garbage, cans, and sign-board etc.

- Keep some wooden boards ready, to shield glass windows.
- Keep hurricane lanterns filled with kerosene, dragon lights, match boxes, candles, and extra dry cells.
- Promptly demolish condemned (unsafe) buildings.
- Those who have radio sets should ensure that the radio is fully serviceable. In case of transistors, an extra set of batteries should be kept handy.
- During cyclone season, keep the overhead water tanks full all the time.
- Elevated hand pumps near shelters can help sustain water shortage during stay in shelters.
- Use modern portable hand operated purification of water gadgets for drinking and cooking purposes.

Steps to be Taken by the Community when Cyclone Warning (24 hours before) is Received

- Keep your radio on and listen to the latest weather warnings and advice from the nearest All India Radio Station. Pass on the information to others. Conserve batteries. Open one or two radios only at a time.
- Avoid being misled by rumours. Pass on only the official information you have got from the radio to others.
- Get away from low - lying areas or other locations, which may be swept by high tides or storm surges. Leave sufficiently early, before your way to high ground gets flooded. Do not delay and run the risk of being marooned.
- If your house is out of danger from high tides, and is well built, it is probably the best place to weather the storm. However act promptly, if asked to evacuate.
- Bolt and board up glass windows or put storm shutter in place. Use good wooden planks to securely fastenup. Provide strong suitable support for outside doors.
- If you do not have wooden boards handy, paste paper strips on glasses to prevent splinters flying into the house.
- Get extra food, specially precooked things by Defence Food Research Laboratory, Mysore, which can be eaten without

cooking or with very little preparation and in some cases without water. Store extra drinking water in suitably covered vessels.

- If you are in one of the evacuation areas, move your valuable articles to upper floors or tie them to the ceiling to minimize flood damage. Carry family kits with you while evacuating.
- Have hurricane lantern with match boxes, flashlights and/or other emergency lights in working condition and keep them ready.
- Check on every thing that might blow away or be torn loose. Kerosene tins, cans, agriculture implements, garden tools, road signs and other objects become weapons of destruction in strong winds. Remove them and store them in covered places.
- Make provision for children, sick and elders requiring special diet/help/medicines.
- If the center or 'eye' of the storm passes directly over your place, there would be a lull in the wind and rain, lasting for half an hour or more. During this period, stay in a safe place. Make emergency repairs during the lull period if necessary, but remember that strong wind would return suddenly from the opposite direction frequently with even greater velocity.
- Be calm. Your ability to meet the emergency would inspire and help others.
- Head for the proper shelter or evacuation points indicated for your area.
- Do not worry about your left - back property, as evacuated areas will be policed. To prevent looting, arrange community policing with help of local police. Persons left for community policing should be healthy and honest.
- At the shelter, follow instructions of the person in charge.
- Remain in shelter until informed that you may leave.
- Keep calm at all times. If instructions are observed promptly, there is little personal danger involved.

Post Cyclone Measures by the Community

After a cyclone passes, the public are advised to take the following safety measures:

- They should remain in shelters until informed by those in charge that they may return home.
- They should get themselves inoculated against diseases immediately at the nearest hospital and seek medical care for the injured and sick.
- Any loose and hanging wire from the lamp post should be strictly avoided. A person should be kept to watch or sign post in local language so that nobody goes near the wire and the nearest electrical authorities should be informed.
- People should keep away from flooded areas, unless it is absolutely necessary.
- Anti - social elements should be prevented from doing mischief.
- Houses and dwellings should be cleared of debris.
- The losses should be reported to the revenue authorities (proforma to be obtained from District Administration).

case study contd...

Case Study

Orissa Super Cyclone 1999

Hazard Profile

The geographical peculiarities of Orissa have made it a continuous victim of the natural hazards. The economic health of the state is purely dependent on vagaries of monsoons and devastating effect of natural calamities. The socio economic condition of the people of Orissa is guided by the interplay of various natural forces. The floods, drought and cyclones are regular features in the history of Orissa. Cyclones cause immense damage to life and property. There is total destruction of crops over wide areas and as an effect of the salt wave (storm surge), huge area of land remains out of cultivation for some years. Orissa coast is one of the four most cyclone and storm surge vulnerable coasts of India. Northern Orissa coast is highly vulnerable to cyclones because of concave shaped coastline which results in serious storm surge problem. The coastal districts of Orissa have been hit by 11 severe cyclones and 56 cyclone storms in the last 125 years with maximum storm surge height varying between 3.2 to 5.5 meters. There are two cyclonic peaks in their occurence, one during May-July and the other during October-November, when maximum cyclones have hit Orissa. A 240 km wide belt in Balasore, Bhadrak, Kendrapara, Jagatsinghpur, Puri, Khurda and Ganjam districts have been identified as cyclone hazard zone.

Super Cyclone

1999 was worst year for Orissa; the state experienced severe floods affecting 8 districts in August 1999. In October, the state bore the brunt of two cyclones, in a gap of just 11 days, which affected 14 districts.

The first cyclone of 17-18 Oct. was a very severe cyclone, with wind speeds reaching 200 kmph, affecting four Southern coastal districts.

The Super Cyclone of 29 October 1999 which whirled through Orissa had originated in Gulf of Siam, passing through Andaman and Nicobar Islands The warm sea temperature (about 26.5 degree celsius) in Bay of Bengal acted as catalyst helping the cyclone to become even more intense as it approached Orissa coast. Since the cyclone spent more time at sea and the temperature of water was more than 27 degree celsius, it turned out to be super cyclone due to favourable atmosphere over Bay of Bengal. It was first sighted on October 25 (Afternoon) in Gulf of Siam (550 km east of Port Blair). It then entered North Andaman Sea, which rapidly intensified into a cyclone storm on 26 October morning. The system further intensified into a severe cyclone storm on morning of October 27, centered at about 750 km south east of Paradip. As the system approached Orissa coast, it intensified into a Super Cyclone at 0230 hours on October 29 and lay centered approximately 90 km south east of Paradip. The super cyclone stalled for 8 hours, 300 km off the coast in the Bay of Bengal and finally hit Orissa coast between Ersama and Balikuda (South-west of Paradip) at 1030 hours on October 29. The landfall took about 2 hours. The diameter of the cyclone was about 200 km and the wind speed of over 260 kmph.

After crossing the coast the system exhibited slow movements, stalled nearly 3 hours at the centroid of the triangle formed by Jagatsinghpur, Kendrapara and Paradip. Attracted by low pressure it moved to Cuttack and further to Kapilas and stalled there at 2130 hours for almost 12 hours. It then inched towards Anandpur and built a cloud mass with a 250 km extent, collecting water vapor on the way. Finally it retreated to Jaipur causing heavy rainfall all the way through Bhadrak to Balasore. The system remained stationary near Bhubneshwar on October 30 and by the evening the Super Cyclone had weakened into a severe cyclone storm and lay 30 km northwest of Bhubneshwar. Though the speed of gale had considerably subsided around noon of October 30, heavy torrential rains continued till the morning of October 31. The cyclone had weakened into a depression over North Orissa coast near Chandbali at 1130 hours on October 31 and dissipated into a well marked low pressure area over the Bay of Bengal at 1200 hours on October 31.

Indian Navy Distributing food to Cyclone affected people

An overturned Helicopter

Severely Damaged Roads and Infrastructure

An uprooted Bridge

Source : www.osdma.com

Table 7.1 : Super Cyclone at a Glance

Landfall Point	**Between Ersama and Balikuda (SW of Paradip)**
Time of Landfall	10.30 AM of October 29, 1999
Storm Surge	7-10 Meters
Eye of the Storm	Paradip
Diameter of Cyclone	200 km
Central Pressure of the Storm	926 hpa (hpa)
Storm Intensity	6.5 in Beuforte scale
Wind Speed	260-300 kmph

Table 7.2 : Effect of Cyclone

Population Affected	1,56,81072
No of Villages Affected	14586
No. of Districts Affected	12
Human Lives lost	9893
Livestock Perished	4,44,531
Houses Damaged	1661683
Cropped Area Damaged (ha)	18,43047
Schools Damaged	18,348

Response

Due to magnitude of impact and extreme severiety of the cyclone, the entire state had paralyzed after the cyclone subsided. All channels of communications had broken down. Satellite telephone sent by Andhra Pradesh Chief Minister to his counterpart in Orissa was of no use as the battery ran out after a few calls and nobody knew how to recharge the battery with the small generator. HAM volunteers from National Institute of Amateur Radio, Hyderabad were the first ones to keep the link alive with outside world. The initial reports of devastation were communicated through HAM radios. This helped in search and rescue and relief in a better manner. Army and Air Force help was requisitioned on 29 October but they were able to undertake operations only on 31 October, due to bad weather. Indian Navy reopened navigation channel of Paradip on 1 November, 1999. This facilitated movement of ships carrying relief material. Flash floods from 31 October onwards hampered rescue operations by the Army. The Government of Andhra Pradesh sent 100 engineers and a number of Rapid Response Teams to clear road blocks and assist in rescue and relief operations. The Army helped in removal of debris and restoring road and rail links. The Air Force, Navy and Territorial Army spearheaded the preliminary relief and rescue efforts. Armed Forces started biggest ever rescue and relief operations under "Operation Sahayata".

Initial relief was provided by Government of Andhra Pradesh and CARE INDIA. Andhra Government sent-satellite phone, relief teams, road clearing team and 500 personnel from APTRANSCO to restore power lines and a team of 50 doctors and 80 paramedics alongwith medicines and relief material. Para mititary/police forces from other states were deployed to assist in the task of relief distribution and maintenance of law and order.

Government of India

National Crises Management Committee met at 2030 hours on 29 October, to take stock of the situation and organise urgent relief measures. The Cabinet Secretary directed concerned central agencies to start providing immediate relief without waiting for a detailed request. Secretary Agriculture, nodal ministry wrote to Chief Secretaries of all States and Union Territories, for their assistance in relief operations. Air Force was asked to provide fixed wing aircrafts and helicopters for air dropping of relief material in affected districts of

Orissa. Army columns moved in to remove fallen trees, power poles, debris and restore road communications. Unified Control Room was established in Agriculture Ministry in Krishi Bhawan, New Delhi. Items like diesel generator (DG) sets, food stuffs, tents, kerosene, match boxes, candles, tarpaulines, medicines/medical teams, telecommunication equipment *etc* were procured and despatched to affected districts. Control Room functioned round the clock. Coordination of NGOs, International Organisations, media *etc* was done in the Control Room. A website was launched for dissemination of latest information. A central team under Additional Secretary, Department of Agriculture and Cooperation (DAC) visited Orissa on 3rd November to make rapid assessment of the damages and requirement of relief and reconstruction. Rs. 100 crore was released from National Calamity Relief Fund. Funds from NCCF and PM Relief Fund were also released. For management of relief at Central level, DAC was made overall incharge. Central Relief Commissioner coordinated the efforts of all line ministries and departments (Telecommunication, Surface Transport, Railways and Power) and international agencies.

Government of Orissa

In the immediate aftermath of cyclone, virtually all essential infrastructure and state machinery was in complete disarray, making it practically impossible to start immediate rescue and relief operations. There were various constraints, for example large stretches of land were inundated. Roads were either submerged or washed away. They were also blocked by uprooted trees and electricity poles. Besides continuous rains till 01 November posed a major stumbling block in carrying emergency relief and rescue. There was complete breakdown of communication channels and disruption of power supply and surface transport. The Chief Minister of Orissa made an appeal to Central Government, all State Governments and international aid agencies to extend humanitarian support to cyclone affected people. The state government machinery was thrown totally out of gear in the initial response period. It however recovered fast with wide ranging support coming from central government, armed forces / para military forces, other state governments, notably Andhra Pradesh, public sector undertakings including insurance and banking sectors, NGOs and international aid agencies. The relief was so much that management of relief distribution posed a major problem. A Central Relief

Coordination Center was set up to coordinate relief work and a NGO Coordination Cell was activated to coordinate the NGO activities. Air and railway entry points were earmarked to receive and account for relief. The relief was initially provided for 15 days as per state relief code. It was continued for another 15 days in critical areas. Air dropping of food continued from 01 to 16 November 1999. Free kitchens were started by voluntary organisations. Drinking water, clothes and shelter material was distributed to cyclone victims. Special Relief Commissioner was coordinating the relief operations and air dropping. House building assistance was distributed. Exgratia assistance to next of kin of victims was given as per state relief code. In addition, Rs. 50,000/- was distributed per person killed in cyclone from Prime Minister Relief Fund. Other actions taken included :

- Establishment of Control Room on midnight of 31 October 1999
- Restoration of vital installations like electricity, water supply sewerage, road, rail *etc.*
- Damage assessment in affected districts in terms of human lives lost, cattle stock lost, buildings, property and agriculture losses.

Response of Armed Forces

In the post cyclone period, Indian Armed Forces emerged with an enhanced reputation, for their quick response, commitment and dedication. Opertion 'Sahayata' was launched, the largest ever relief and rescue effort in the Indian History. A total of 35 Army columns were deployed which started functioning from 01 November 1999. The first Navy ship carrying edible material, candles and match boxes left Vishakhapattnam on 31 October. Armed Forces also restored telecommunication and transporation infrastructure. Distribution of relief material and air dropping of food material and other essential items were carried out by them. Indian Navy rushed in relief to Paradip port, for further distribution.

Para Military Forces Response

21 companies of para military forces (CRPF, CISF, RAF) were deployed to assist State Government in relief distribution and maintenance of law and order. In addition, 10 medical teams of para military forces were deployed. Armed police forces of other states were also utilised to maintain the civic order and distribution of relief material.

Response of United Nations (UN) and International Non Governmental Organisations (NGOs)

UN and international NGOs launched a massive relief and rehabilitation program. UN sanctioned US $50 million for relief, rehabilitation and reconstruction work in next 15 years. UN Disaster Management team landed after two days. It ensured working in close coordination with national control room at Bhubneshwar. WHO was designated as focal point for providing technical support. UNICEF was coordinating international relief and World Food Project (WFD) coordinated efforts of NGOs like CARE, OXFAM & ACTION AID. UNDP helped preparing blue print for disaster resistant houses. UNFPA, the FPO, ILO, and WHO formed a sub group to focus attention on medium and long term rehabilitation and reconstruction needs. A comprehensive exercise was carried out which was updated from time to time. The map indicated affected areas which were covered under relief and areas which were left out for other agencies to work on. Media was kept informed to avoid duplication of efforts.

Response of NGOs / Volunteer Organisations

Many NGOs came for help with manpower and material. A NGO Coordination Cell was created. They moved into remote areas. In fact local NGOs formed into one group and were the first to respond when government machinery was rendered non functional. They ran free kitchens, drinking water, medicines, shelter material, disposal of dead bodies, in a concerted manner. Orissa Disaster Mitigation Mission was formed to identify different role players for intervention.

Public Sector Companies

Public Sector companies all over the country made significant contribution towards relief. They adopted various blocks in affected districts. The Housing and Urban Development Corporation (HUDCO) initiated programs for reconstruction, repair, renewal and retrofitting damaged and vulnerable houses, with focus on weaker sections.

The nation as a whole stood behind Orissa with housewives, children and even weaker segment of people coming forward with monetary and in kind help.

Rehabilitation

Due to huge loss of human lives, a number of women became widows and many children were orphaned. Rehabilitation measures were required to incorporate special needs of this section of society. Social security benefits, sustained means of shelter and nutrition were required to be provided. 1500 orphans needed special attention. Their health needs had to be catered for, as they were more prone to diseases. The survivors also needed trauma counseling and psychological help.

Restoration of Livelihood

- *Agriculture Sector :* Since most of agricultural fertile land had been damaged, crops and plantation destroyed, unemployed agricultural labour needed to be rehabilitated. 'Food for work' was started. Coconut plantation had been completely destroyed. People depending on plantation needed to be given alternate short term means of livelihood.
- *Livestock :* As a secondary means of income, the loss of livestock has had a serious repercussion on rural economy. Rehabilitation of livestock needed to be given a prominent place due to its impact on the increased earning of the community. As a mitigation measure, fodder stock and shelter for cattle were essential for such contingencies.
- *Fishing Sector :* Catching fish requires means and implements that had been lost in the cyclone. The fishermen were required to be provided boats and fishing nets for rehabilitation. It took time to rehabilitate them.
- *Small scale and Household Industry :* A total of 2270 small scale industries and 1238 primary units were affected. Raw material and markets were provided to the rural employment sector.
- *Houses :* More than two million houses were destroyed. Assistance in terms of loans and monetary doles were given with trained artisans to reconstruct and rebuild the houses.
- *Infrastructure :* Water, electricity, irrigation system were severely affected. It took time and efforts to restore them.
- *Public and School Buildings :* 18059 public buildings and 20141 school buildings were damaged. School buildings were given priority. Schools were reopened in tents. Cyclone shelters were made to provide shelter during future cyclones.
- *Communication System :* Communication system like rail and road network took time for restoration. Communications were given priority for restoration.

- *Environmental Issues* : 90 million trees had been damaged and 90% trees were uprooted in affected districts. Mangrove forests in Kendrapara and Jagatsinghpur districts were destroyed. Social forestry program and regeneration of mangrove and coastal shelter belt plantation was taken up. Strip plantation was done beyond 10 km from coast towards inland to help as wind barriers. OXFAM, ODMM, LWS and World Vision helped in rehabilitation of environment.

Disaster Management Planning and Capacity Building

A comprehensive disaster management and hazard mitigation system was put in place. It involved detailed multi hazard vulnerability, risk and capacity assessment, fully developed long term multihazard disaster prepardness and mitigation plan, fully developed communication system and network, warning dissemination system and network at district, block and village level, construction of multipurpose cyclone shelters and cattle shelters with management plan, community participation in disaster management by raising teams of disaster preparedness volunteers, institutional capacity building, long term multi hazard public awareness program, micro finance credit scheme for retrofitting of houses and community based disaster mitigation *etc.* The detailed study was funded by DFID. The Orissa State Disaster Management Authority (OSDMA) was created to undertake comprehensive restoration and reconstruction program for revival of intrastructure and economy and also to prepare the state for handling such disasters better in future. The Chief Minister is head of OSDMA and a senior bureaucrat is its Chief Executive Officer.

Orissa Super Cyclone was a catastrophe for which the state was not prepared. Its aftermath raised many issues and these were addressed and set the pace for better disaster management in India.

Chapter 8

Avalanches

Introduction

Road traffic in cold snowy regions during winter season faces problems, like icing of road, snow compaction and snow storms that obstruct visibility. In snowy region there is also danger of damage due to snow avalanches. Avalanches often severely damage road service facilities or road structures. Quick response and corrective actions are required to cope with the damages, if any avalanche occurs.

Causes of Avalanches

General Concept : Snow cover on slope tends to slide down the slope because of gravity. Conditions affecting stability include the gravitational force component of the snow and resisting forces, such as the frictional resistance of the slope or the anchoring effect of shrubs. In general, avalanches are caused when this balance is lost and when the forces exceed the resistance. Avalanches are rarely observed closely since they normally occur during a short time period of one to two minutes.

Major Causes : Major causes can be classified into fixed (prime factors) and variable factors (exciting factors), such as weather conditions and the weight of the snow cover. Avalanches occur when these factors are combined. The types and scales of avalanches differ depending on the combination of these various factors and their scale.

Fig. 8.1: How Avalanches are Formed

Fig. 8.2 : Fracture in Cornice

Primary Factors

Topographic

- Inclination of slope where avalanche occurs. More inclined the slope, more chances of its occurrence.
- Scale of Slope.
- Shape of Slope.
- Location (ridge line or toe of the slope)
- Orientation of slope.

Vegetation

- Vegetation cover and height of trees.
- Vegetation cover and its thickness.

Exciting or Variable Factors

Weather

- Depth of snow cover.
- Depth of snowfall.
- Wind velocity.
- Atmospheric and snow temperatures.

Other Factors

- Increase in weight of snow cover because of snow dropping from cornices or snow cover.
- Vibrations such as earthquake or the sound of gunfire or even movement of large No. of personnel making noises.

Types of Avalanches

- There are different types of avalanches. They vary depending on the mechanism, the conditions and time of occurrence and the type of movement. The factors such as causes, conditions at the time of occurrence and type of movement must be taken into account in classifying avalanches which are as follow:

Fig. 8.3 : Loose Snow of Avalanche

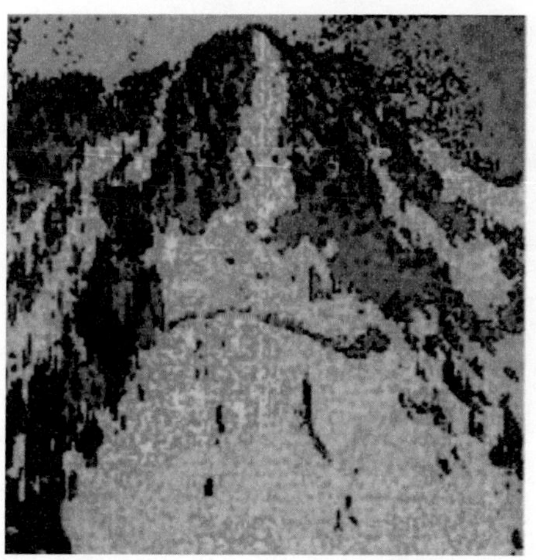

Fig. 8.4 : Slab Snow Avalanche

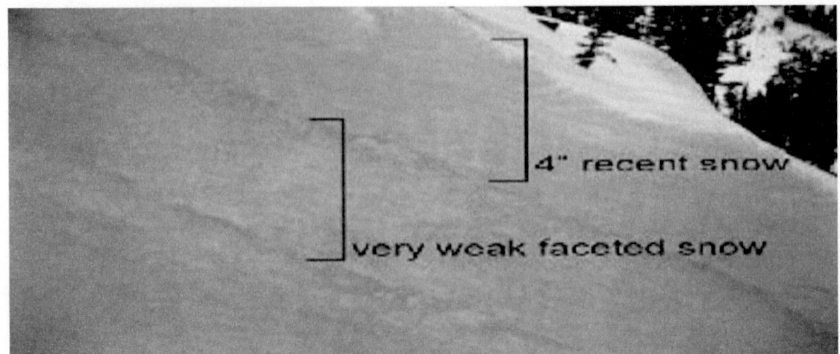

Fig. 8.5 : Weak Snow Pack

Table 8.1 : Various Types of Avalanches

Classification Factor	Type of Avalanches	Definition
Type of Occurrence	Loose Snow Avalanche	Avalanches that flow rapidly, spreading widely from a point, normally small in scale.
	Slab Avalanches	Avalanches that start to move suddenly over wide areas, normally large in scale.
Type of Snow	Dry Snow Avalanche	Avalanche that contain no water.
	Wet Snow Avalanche	Avalanche that contain water.
Location of slip surface	Surface Layer Avalanche	Slip surface exist within the snow cover.
	Full Depth Avalanche	Slip surface occurs on the ground surface.

Types of Damages Due to Snow Avalanche

- Traffic is blocked by snow deposited on road surfaces.
- Road surface is damaged by avalanches.
- Road structure, such as retaining walls, are overturned.
- During road construction, avalanches cause more destruction.

Avalanche Control Measures

Types of Control Measures – Avalanche control measures can roughly be classified into hardware and software types. Hardware measures are for the purpose of preventing avalanches or for blocking or deflecting avalanches with protective structures. Software measures provide safety by eliminating the probability of avalanches by removing snow deposit or slope with blasting and by predicting the occurrence of avalanches and recommending evacuation from hazardous areas.

Avalanche Control Structures

Avalanche control structures can be divided into two major types

- Preventive Structures.
- Protection Structures.

Preventive Structure

- *Planting (Avalanche Prevention Forest) :* Avalanche prevention forest protect snow cover from movement by the resistance of tree trunks and branches, increase the stability of snow cover by uniformly distributing it and control quick changes in snow cover.
- *Stepped Terraces :* Stepped terraces are provided for stabilizing snow cover on slopes by reducing or dividing the sliding force of snow cover with steps in the slopes. Steps are easy to construct at reasonable cost but are not effective in controlling surface layer avalanches.
- *Avalanches Control Piles :* These are assembly of single piles driven into slopes in avalanche zones to control surface layer avalanches. Type of snow should determine the spacing of piles or topographic features. An average spacing of 5 metres is used.
- *Avalanches Control Fence :* Strong fence is installed on slopes of avalanche zone to prevent full depth or surface layer avalanches.
- *Suspended Fence :* These are used in steep slopes or in areas where foundations cannot be properly installed because of poor ground conditions and are useful in small areas.
- *Snow Cornice Control Structures :* These structures are installed at top of mountain areas to prevent development of snow cornices that can cause avalanches. There are two methods of prevention, one is a collector snow fence which collects snow on the windward side of the top of the mountain, and the other is a blower snow fence which controls the development of snow cornice by blocking winds on the ridge.

Protection Structures

Protective structures are installed in the avalanche path or in snow deposit areas to change the flow direction of avalanches (deflecting structures) to accentuate their energy (retarding structures), to block their flow or to allow their passage (protecting structures)

- *Protecting Fences :* They are provided to block the flow of avalanches, similar to the action of retaining walls. They are usually constructed of steel and are used mainly for blocking small avalanches.
- *Retaining Walls :* Installed in snow deposit areas to block flow of avalanches before they reach the roadside. These walls need pockets to absorb the snow deposited by avalanches and are not effective unless they are installed on gentle slopes of 20 degree or less.
- *Deflecting Structures :* They change the flow direction of avalanches to eliminate interference to road traffic. They can be deflecting walls, fences, banks, channels and avalanche wedges.
- *Snow Sheds :* It is a roofed structure installed over a road to allow the flow of an avalanche over the roof. This is most reliable of the various avalanche protection measures.
- *Retarding Structure :* These are structures to reduce the flow velocity or the scale of the avalanche. These are of various types, such as earth mounds, retarding piles, grating crib work and retarding fences.

Other Control Measures

Prediction and Forecasting : Prediction of avalanches cannot only prevent avalanche disasters but can also make it efficiently dispose off dangerous snow deposits and cornices.

Disposal of Avalanches Potential Snow Packs : Methods that dispose off snow packs on hazardous slopes include hand labour, mechanical methods that use blasting powder. In general small avalanches are disposed off by hand or mechanical methods while large avalanches are disposed off by blasting.

Chapter 9

Forest Fires

Introduction

Forests face many hazards but most common is forest fire. They pose threat to not only forest wealth but also to entire region of fauna and flora seriously disturbing the bio-diversity, ecology and environment of a region. During summer, forests are littered with dry senescent leaves and twigs which could burst into flames ignited by the slightest spark. Forest cover in India is 675,538 km and constitute 20-25% of geographical area.

Fig. 9.1 : Natural Forest Fires

Fig. 9.2 : Controlled Forest Fires

Classification of Forest Fires

There are *three categories of forest fires :*

a) Natural or controlled forest fires.

b) Forest fires caused by heat generated in the litter and other biomes in summer due to carelessness of people (human neglect).

c) Forest fires purposely caused by local inhabitants.

Types of Fires

Forest fire differs depending upon its nature, size, spreading speed, behaviour *etc*. Depending on nature and size these can be grouped into four types as follows :

Underground Fires : Low intensity fires consuming organic matter beneath the surface litter of forest floor. They occur in wettier part of mountains. A thick mantle of organic matter is found on top of the mineral soil. Fire spreads consuming such material burns for months and destroy vegetative cover of the soil. It is also known as MUCK FIRE.

Surface Fires : Most common, fire burns undergrowth and dead material along the floor. Useful for forest growth and regeneration. If it grows in size, the fire engulfs undergrowth and middle storey of the forest.

Ground Fires : There is no clear distinction between underground and ground fire. After smouldering for sometime, underground fire change into ground fire. This fire burns roots and other material on or beneath the surface. They are more damaging than surface fires as they can destroy vegetation completely. Ground fires burn underneath the surface by smouldering combustion and are most often ignited by surface fires. These fires are often hard to detect and are the least spectacular and slowest moving, fighting them is very difficult and tedious.

Crown Fires : They are most unpredictable fires which burn the top of trees and spread rapidly by winds. They are generally ignited by surface fires. Crown fires burn top to top of trees or shrubs, more or less independently, of the surface fires. Since such fires are over the heads of the ground forces, they are uncontrollable until they drop to the ground. Fire fighters can get trapped and die. A crown fire is particularly very dangerous in a coniferous forest because resinous material released by ignited logs burn furiously. On hill slopes, if the fire starts downhill it spreads fast as heated air adjacent to a slope tends to flow up the slope spreading flames alongwith it. If the fire starts uphill, there is less likelihood of it spreading downwards.

Causes of Fire

Casual Factors

- Deliberate igniting by small scale farmers.
- Slash and burn shifting cultivation.
- Need for fodder for grazing of animals.
- Production of tendu leaves.
- Mahua Flower.

Natural Causes

- Lightning
- In dry season, friction leading to sparks by rolling stones in mountainous area.
- In bamboo areas, rubbing together of clums of dry bamboos.
- Volcanic eruption.

Accidental Causes

- Heat accumulation in dry heaps of leaves during hot summer.
- Un-extinguished camp fires of trekkers, labour camps, nomads with their animals, fires of road side charcoal panniers when not put out properly.
- Sparks generated from railway engines, mainly steam locomotives.
- Missing sparks from the trucks/vehicles.
- Careless throwing of cigarettes, biddi stubs, match sticks by graziers.
- Careless burning of fields after harvesting the crops.
- Careless handling of resin during resin tapping in summer season.

Fig. 9.3 : Dousing of fire by aircraft

DO'S & DON'TS

What to do before, during and after a forest fire

- In case living in forest, build an underground area which should be well stocked including water. In case forest fire is detected move to basement and stay there till normalcy returns.
- Forest officials, local people and tribals living in forests should play a constructive role, before, during and after the forest fire.
- To keep the sources of fire or source of ignition separate from combustible and inflammable material.
- Nothing should come up in fire lanes in forest areas.
- Try to maintain forest blocks to prevent dry litter from piling up in forests during summer season.
- Try to put the fire out by digging or circle around it with water. If not possible, call for a fire tender from nearest fire and emergency services.
- Move farm animals and movable goods to safer places.
- During fire, listen regularly to radio for advance information and obey the instructions cum advice.
- Follow the effective monitoring and warning systems including remote sensing.
- To adopt safe practices in areas near forests especially by factories, coal mines, oil stores, chemical plants and even household kitchens.

- To incorporate fire reducing and fire fighting techniques and equipment while planning a building or coal mining operation.
- In case of forest fires the volunteer teams are essential not only for fire fighting but also to keep watch on the start of the forest fire and a sound alert system.
- Teach the causes and harm of fire to your family and others.
- Do not be scared when a sudden fire occurs in the forest; be calm and encourage others of the community to overcome the problem patiently.
- Do apply seasonal mitigation measures *i.e.* fuel reduction.
- To arrange fire fighting drills frequently. Training of personnel in fire fighting.
- To keep the source of fire under watch and control.
- Community/school/family to teach children not to throw cigarattes/bidi butts and burn casual fires in forests.
- Community near forest area to keep watch on forest fires on volentary basis from elevated towers to be constructed by forest department.

What one should Not Do

- One should not throw smouldering cigarette butt or bidi in the forests.
- Picnickers should not leave the burning wood sticks.
- Do not enter the forest during the fire.
- Do not leave dry litter during summer season.
- Tribals should not use slash and burn method of farming indiscriminately on large scale.
- Do not run away from fire, it is likely to catch you and chances of survival would be difficult.

Chapter 10

Tsunami

What is Tsunami ?

- Tsu-nami is a Japanese word. Tsu-means 'harbour' and 'nami' means 'wave'. In earlier times the Japanese fishermen on return to coast from sea voyage found devastation when nothing happened to them at sea and hence named it Tsunami.
- They are called tidal waves but they have actually nothing to do with the tides. However their appearance from shore is similar to rapidly rising or falling tides.
- Tsunami are long waves- some times with hundreds of miles between their crests, just like the concentric waves generated by an object dropped into a pool.
- Tsunami is gravity wave system, triggered by vertical disturbance in the ocean like earthquake, landslide or volcanic eruption.
- In deep sea open waters, waves are not noticed as they rise not more than a few inches but speed upto 800 km per hour. When

depth decreases in shallow waters of the shore, wave length gets shortened and the height of waves increases. Waves crush into shore with tremendous power to wreck buildings and throw trucks like ping pong balls.

The Tsunamis have a trick or so up their watery sleeves. If TROUGH of the wave hits shore before the CREST, the first thing one notices on shore is not water rushing onto land, but the opposite. Sea rushes out, so beaches become magically full of colourful fishes. The water disappears upto 300-400 meters off the coast. The tendency of people to run and catch the fish should be avoided as the following wave/s may take away the onlookers with them.

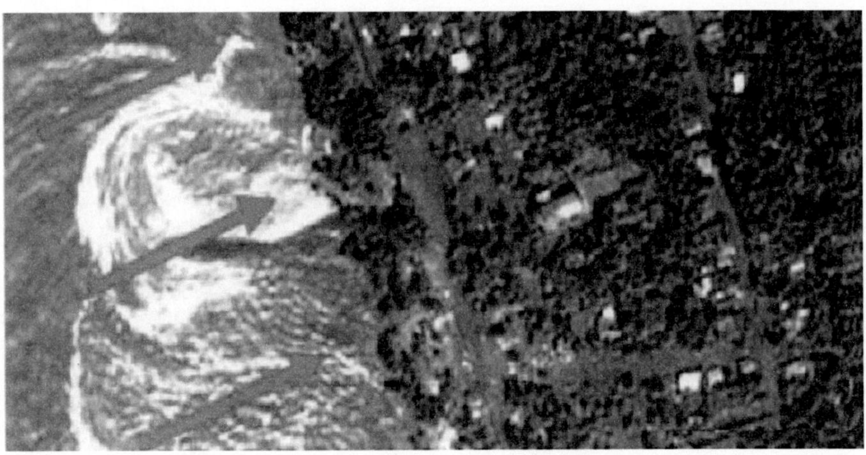

Fig. 10.1 : During Indian Ocean Tsunami 2004, several waves of tsunami came at intervals of between 5 and 40 minutes. In Kalutara, Srilanka the water reached at least 1 km (0.6 miles) inland, causing widespread destruction.
Source : NOAA, USGS.

Effects of Tsunami

- *Inundation :* The sea water inundates from 300 meters to 3 km inside the coast line and causes havoc.
- *Waves Impact on Structures :* The waves destroy any structure that come their way. The destruction to infrastructure is usually very heavy.
- *Erosion :* Tsunami waves move back as fast as they approach and cause erosion to the existing structures, especially the foundations.

Fig. 10.2 : Immediate Effect of Tsunami Waves

Fig. 10.3 : Structures being hit by Tsunami Waves

Fig. 10.4 : Tsunami Waves Causing Erosion

Causes of Tsunami Triggering

There are four main causes of triggering Tsunami. These are given in succeeding paras.

Tectonic Movement

When an Earthquake of the magnitude of 7.5 and above, on the Richter scale, hits the floor of the sea, the earthquake is caused due to movement of tectonic plates and release of stored energy.

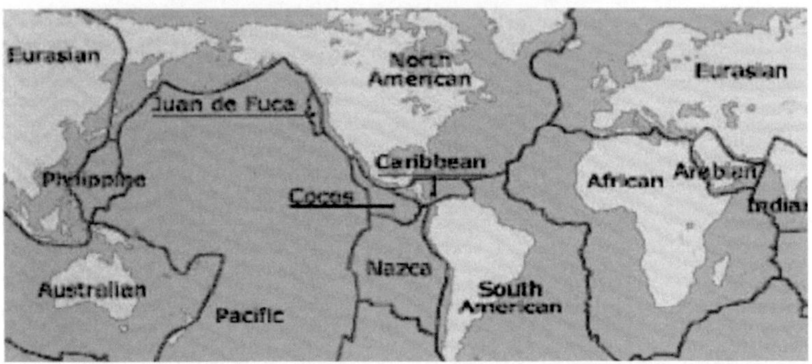

Fig. 10.5 : Most earthquakes occur along the edges of the Earth's plates.

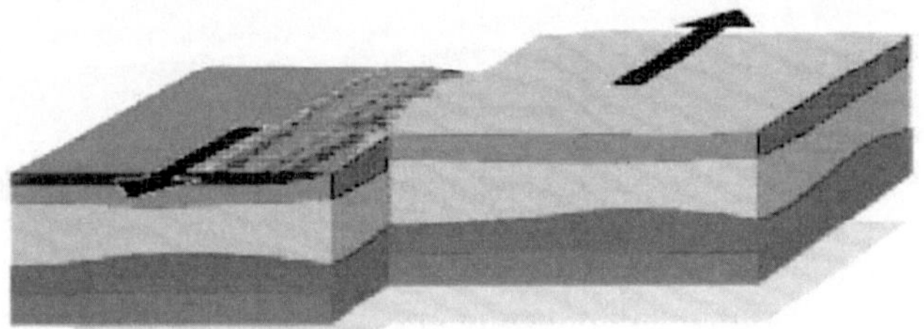

Fig. 10.6 : Earthquakes occur when parts of two tectonic plates move suddenly against each other.

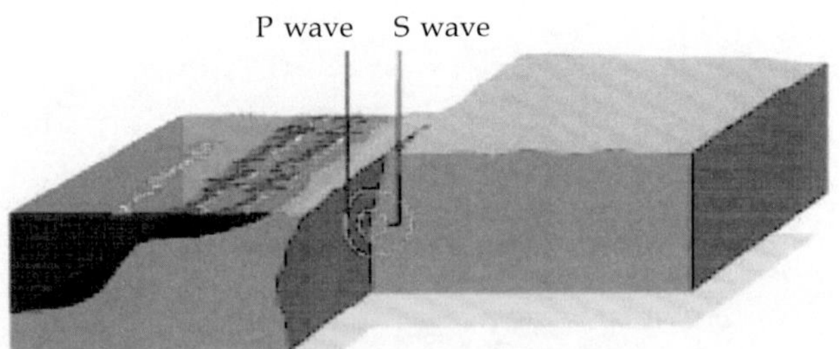

Fig. 10.7 : Earthquakes can be detected by different types of waves they generate. The 'P' or primary wave travels fastest through the centre of the earth while the 'S' or secondary wave moves slowly but causes more damage.

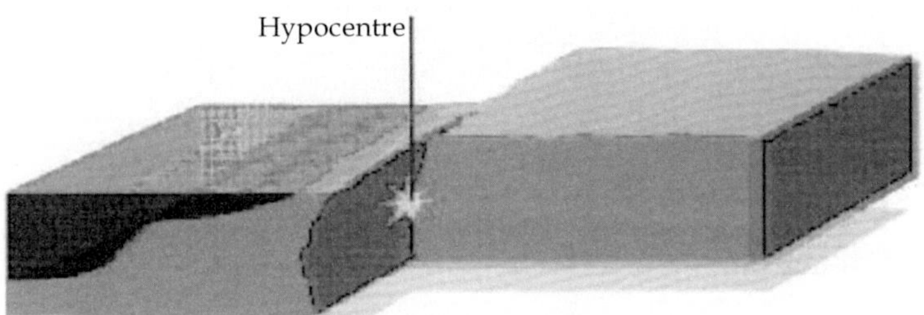

Fig. 10.8 : The rocks usually break deep underground at the focus or hypocentre. This causes the earth or sea above to shake violently.

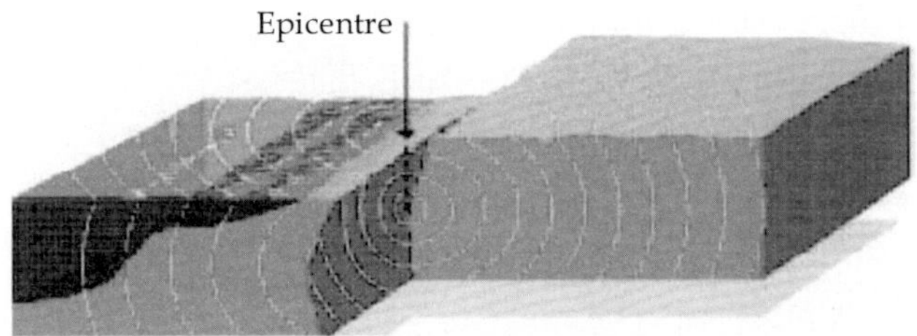

Fig. 10.9 : Waves also spread from the epicentre, the point on the surface above the hypocentre. If an earthquakes occurs under the sea, it can cause a tsunami or tidal wave that spreads for thousands of miles.

Volcanic Eruption

When an undersea volcanic eruption takes place that creates enormous force.

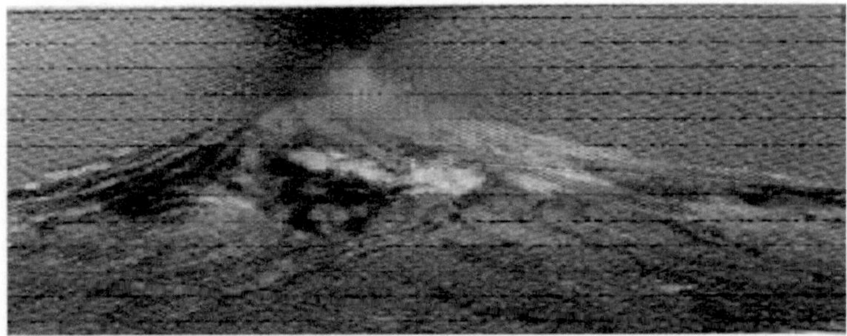

Fig. 10.10 : Undersea volcanic eruptions that create tremendous force.

Meteorite Strike

When a meteorite or an alien force impact the ocean area, disturbing the water from above, tsunami is caused.

Fig. 10.11 : Meteorite impact disturbing the water from above.

Landslide

When a large scale landslide is caused in the mountains in the sea, tsunami is caused and its effect is felt at bays.

Fig. 10.12 : Landslides is Sea Affecting Bays

Protection Against Tsunami

If you are near the coast (300-500 meters from coast line) and experience strong earthquake, just rush out of coastal area and head for high ground (minimum 8-10 meters). If there is a cyclone shelter, or concrete structure nearby, move into its first or second floor.

If the early warning system against Tsunami is in position, the Seismological Stations will detect any earthquake. Earthquake with intensity of more than 7.5 on Richter Scale will be taken note of. The Tide Station will monitor forming of any wave subsequently. However, every time an earthquake of more than 7.5 on Richter Scale takes place, it is not necessary that Tsunami wave will follow automatically. Hence, Tidal Stations watch the appearance of wave after the earthquake. For example on 28 March 2005, an earthquake of the magnitude of

8.3 on the richter scale had hit the same area of Indian Ocean near Sumatara where Tsunami of 26 December 2004 had originated, but this time no Tsunami wave appeared.

If you get caught in a Tsunami, due to lesser or no warning, cling on to a stable object like a tree or a pole and do not leave it till the retreating wave has gone back. The chances of survival are more if you also try and hold your breath, so that you do not swallow dirt and salty sea water.

There should be no infrastructure / houses upto 500 meters from the coastline.

Warning System

When an earthquake of more than 7.5 on Richter scale is detected by sensors, placed on the surface of the sea floor, Tsunami Watch is issued.

If Tidal Stations confirm a follow up wave, Tsunami Warning follows. Precise time at different points on the coast can be predicted but the height of waves, its size and duration cannot be gauzed.

The Warning is lifted after an area is clear of dangerous waves for two hours, or more.

Monitoring Tsunami

Tsunami waves can be detected accurately by planting sensors on the floor of the sea. This has been depicted in Fig. 10.13.

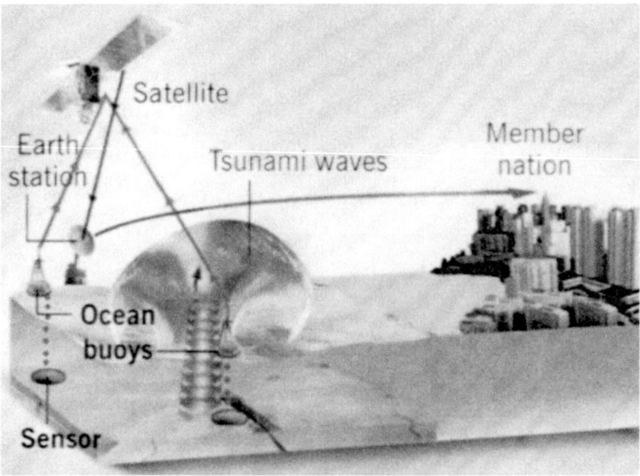

Fig. 10.13 : A Tsunami warning system in place

The underwater sensors monitor and pick up the signals of earthquake and pass information to the floating buoy/ Tsunami Processing Center, who in turn relay it to the designated satellite. The Satellite convey the message to Tsunami Warning Centre/ Earth Stations. The Centre/ Station broadcast the approaching danger to the people through print and electronic media.

Characteristics of Tsunami

- There is no effect of Tsunami on the surface of the sea, even if you are only half to one kilometer away from coast.
- Tsunami may come in waves, with a time gap of 40 minutes to one hour between successive major waves. In one major wave, there may be up to ten sub waves.
- Although the speed of the approaching Tsunami waves at coast gets reduced from 700-800 km to 50-60 km per hour, they carry enormous energy.
- The height of waves at coast can go upto 50 to 70 feet. At point of origin, although there is a large scale displacement of water, the increase in wave length is a few inches only.
- The retreating Tsunami waves are as quick and as dangerous as in their approach and cause as much damage.
- Major devastation is restricted upto 1000 meters inland.
- Tsunami causes more havoc along beaches which have ocean thousands of meter deep, near the coast. In comparison, if the shallow water extends to more than 100 km, the effect will be that much less. Bangladesh was saved by Tsunami waves, due to the coast configuration.
- If you are caught in a Tsunami wave due to inadequate /little warning, try to hold on to a stable object like tree/ pole.
- Hold your breath while the approaching/ retreating wave pass over, to avoid dirt and sea water choking your body system.

India has put in place Tsunami warning system in Indian Ocean and it is functional.

☛ If you feel a strong earthquake while in beaches/coastal area, leave the area immediately and head for high ground.

Case Study

Indian Ocean Tsunami - 2004

What is Tsunami

Tsunami is a Japanese word meaning 'harbour wave'. Tsunamis are popularly called tidal waves but they actually have nothing to do with the tides. These waves, which affect distant shores, originate from undersea or coastal seismic activity, landslides and volcanic eruptions. Whatever the cause, the sea water is displaced with a violent motion and swells up, ultimately surging overland with great destructive power.

Causes of Tsunami

The geological movements that cause tsunamis are produced in three major ways. The most common of these is fault movement on the sea floor, accompanied by an earthquake. A fault is defined as a planar zone of weakness passing through the earth's crust. The second most common cause of tsunami is a landslide, either occuring underwater or originating above the sea and then plunging into water. The highest tsunami waves reported were produced by a landslide at Lituya Bay, Alaska in 1958.

The third major cause of tsunami is volcanic activity. The flank of a volcano, located near the shore or under water, may be uplifted or depressed similar to action of a fault. Or, the volcano may actually explode. In 1883 the violent explosion of the Krakatoa Volcano in Indonesia, produced tsunamis measuring 40 metres which crashed upon Java and Sumatra killing 36,000 people.

Characteristics

Tsunamis differ from ordinary ocean waves, which are produced by wind blowing over water. Normal waves are rarely longer than 300 metres from crest to crest. Tsunamis, may measure 150 km between successive wave crests. Tsunamis travel much faster than ordinary waves. Compared to normal wave speed of around 100 km per hour, tsunamis in deep waters may travel 800 km per hour and yet increase in water height of only 30-45 cm and often pass unnoticed by ships at sea. Contrary to belief, tsunami is not a single giant wave. It is possible for a tsunami to consist of 10 or more waves, which is termed 'tsunami wave train'. The waves follow each other between 5 and 90 minutes apart. As the waves approach the shore, they travel progressively slower. The final wave speed depends upon the water depth. Waves in 18 metres of depth travel about 50 kmph. The shape of the near shore seafloor influences how tsunamis will behave. Where the shore drops off quickly into the deep water, the waves will be smaller. Areas with shallow shelves, such as the major Hawaiian Islands allow formation of very high waves. In the bays and estuaries, the water may rock back and forth (called seiches) and can amplify waves to some of the greatest heights ever observed. Flooding may extend inland by 500 to 2000 metres.

The Earthquake of 26 December 2004

A series of earthquakes occured in the western coast area of Northern Sumatra, Andaman and Nicobar Islands on 26 December 2004. The two strongest earthquakes had the magnitude of 9.3 on the Richter Scale (3.30 North, 95.78 East, off western coast of Northern Sumatra) and 7.3 on the Richter Scale (6.90 North, 92.95 East in Nicobar Islands). This area is historically prone to seismic upheavals due to its location on the margin of tectonic plates (referred to in Pacific ocean basin as the Ring of Fire). The two plates (Burma and India Plates) which normally grind against each other moving North East 6 cm a year, slid about 15 meters at once, dislocating over 2000 km. length. In next three days there were 68 after shocks which continued to occur even after 6 months. The sudden movement of the plates and subsequent release of stresses caused the earthquakes. The epic centre was more than 5.5 miles below the sea bed. The sea floor overlaying the thrust fault would have uplifted by several metres as a result of the earthquake. This would have forced the water upwards. A series of waves rushed in all directions and raced across the surface towards the shore line moving at 800 kmph.

15 minutes after the earthquake, geophysicist on duty at Pacific Tsunomi Warning Centre in Honolulu, despatched a lukewarm bulletin to Pacific Rim countries, including Thailand and Indonesia,

giving location of earthquake but also expecting no tsunami. After 50 minutes, the bulletin was upgraded indicating tsunami threat. In Indonesia, people saw upgraded bulletin only on 27 December (26 December being Sunday). In Thailand, the duty officer did not inform superiors and was busy answering calls from affected people. No urgency was shown by these two Pacific rim countries. In India and Sri Lanka, tsunami reached after 2 and 3 hours but no warning was given to people. 12 countries were affected and the tsunami waves hit the shores of countries as follows :

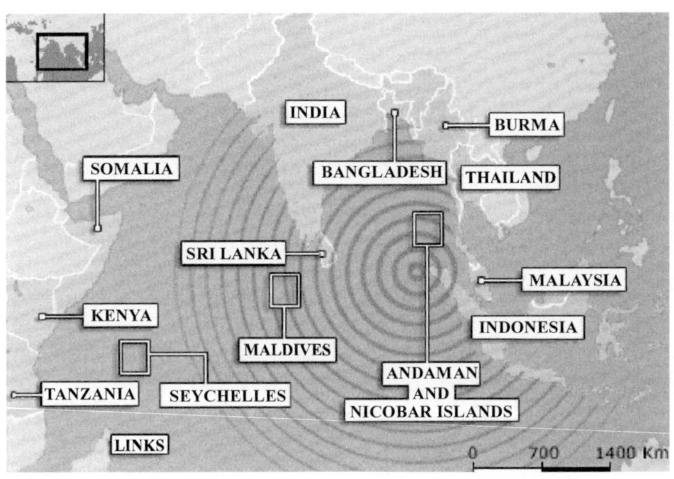

Epicentre	**0058 hrs (GMT)**
❒ Sumatra	+ 15 minutes
❒ Nicobar Islands	+ 30 minutes
❒ Thailand	+ 90 minutes
❒ Sri Lanka	+ 120 minutes
❒ Indian East & South Coast	+ 120 to 150 minutes
❒ Maldives	+ 210 minutes
❒ Somalia	+ 420 minutes

The speed of the tsunami initially was 750-800 kmph and when it hit coast it was between 35-40 kmph. The height of the tsunami waves was 10 metres to 20 metres. The flood waters came inland from 300 metres to 2 km. The basic statistics of the event were as follows :

Region & Country	Off the coast of Northern Sumatra, Indonesia
Moment Magnitude	9.3 on Richter Scale
Date	December 26, 2004
Time	06.28:53 AM (IST), 00:58:53 (UTC)

Epicentre	3.267°N, 95.821°E, near coast of Sumatra
Affected Countries	Indonesia, Sri Lanka, India, Thailand, Somalia, Maldives, Malaysia, Bangladesh, Kenya, Myanmar, Singapore and Seychelles
Casualties	Over 2,80,000

How Powerful Was it?

Waves

- 20 M high waves, travelling 750 kmph-with unimaginable energy.

Earthquake

- Boiling 1000 litres of water for each person on earth
- Production 9,40,000 barrels oil / day for one year
- 13 times the Krakatoa eruption in 1883
- 40,000 'little boys' - the bomb dropped at Hiroshima in Japan in 1945
- 1 Billion of lightening
- 2 exajoules or 2×10^{18} joules.

Tsunami in India

Characteristics

- First time in living memory, tsunami struck Indian Coasts. Last time was in 1942.
- 50% of people in the coastal areas felt earthquake tremors around 6:30 AM.
- There were three main waves of tsunami, with time gap of 10 to 30 minutes. First and third waves caused maximum damage.
- Height of waves varied from 10 to 35 feet. Retreating tsunami waves were as quick and as dangerous as their approach and caused as much damage.
- Tsunami caused more havoc along beaches which had deep ocean depth, just a few km from the coast like in Sri Lanka. Bangladesh was saved as its shallow water extends more than 160 km.
- Fishermen sailing in sea even ½ km from coast did not feel the effects of tsunami.

- People who climbed up trees or held on to some stable object like poles survived.
- 40% of all casualties were children.
- Floating population comprised 35% of all casualities, mostly in Nagapattinam distinct of Tamil Nadu.
- Villages located on high ground (10 metres) even near the coast were spared of the disaster.
- Effect of tsunami on villages behind mangroves and coastal plantation was minimal.
- Effect of tsunami on the villages adjacent to back waters was less.
- People did not receive any tsunami warning.
- All thatched roof huts upto 500 metres from coast were completely destroyed. Single storey brick houses and compound walls were damaged extensively. Not much damage was caused to concrete buildings.
- People did not make use of cyclone shelters, existing near the coast in villages, thinking that they were meant for cyclones and not tsunami.

Search, Rescue and Relief

- Community as in other disasters was the first to respond.
- District administration took 2-3 days to organize themselves as most officials themselves were affected. They however took full control of events after three days and thereafter relief operations were pressed in full swing.
- Armed Forces took over search and rescue and provided relief in Andaman and Nicobar Islands.
- Neighbouring district administration officals came to the rescue of affected districts in the State.
- Over 200 NGOs including international ones came for help. NGO efforts however flowers not optimised.
- The relief initially was not organised properly. People sent old and unused clothes like pants & woolens. No one initially thought of sending lungis for men and dhotis for women. No undergarments, especially for women were sent. Fishermen are

proud people and they did not accept old cothes. Piles of clothes on the roads hindered relief work.

- General awareners about disasters was lacking among people both in preparedness & response.

Rehabilitation

- Most affected were fishermen community and they did not have any alternate profession to fall back upon.
- Most boats and fishing nets were destroyed.
- There was requirement of over one lac boats and 5 lac fishing nets. No Indian company could make them in short period and hence fishermen remained unemployed and could not be rehabilitated. Fibreglass boats were later procured and given to affected families. This raised their income as also standard of living.

Reconstruction

- Most fishermen were living on Govt or unauthorised land (within 500 metres of coast-line)
- Permanent structures could come up only on acquired land which took time. Local community was not ready to accommodate fishing community, due to their food and living habits and social customs. They wanted to keep them away.
- It was decided to build multi hazard resistant houses, 1-2 km from the sea coast.
- Temporary shelters were provided in situ in short period.

Constraints of the Administration

- There was panic. People fled even from unaffected areas in the towns/villages.
- Communications failed and hence it was difficult to marshal people and coordinate the rescue and relief work.
- Piling of boats/superstructures hindered search and rescue operations.
- Damage to roads and buildings caused obstruction to search and rescue teams.
- Hospitals near the coast were inundated and some ICUs and many wards became non-functional.

- Most officials were themselves affected. It took time for them to report back for duty as they were busy looking after their families and property.
- It was a Sunday and post Christmas holiday. Most people were on leave. It took time to form search and rescue and relief teams and deploy them.
- Buses and light vehicles were available but drivers had fled away.
- Fear of another tsunami kept community away from responding. There was hold up in rescue work.
- Electricity and water supply were badly affected. Rescue was confined to day light hours. Water was however restored within 3 days and electricity within 7 days.
- Shopkeepers closed their shops due to fear of arson, which created temporary scarcity.
- Everyone was surprised and caught unawares. It took sometime for them to realise what had hit them. Cause and magnitude was not clear.

The most important lesson of Tsunami 2004 was capacity of India to manage a major natural disaster on its own. India did not seek help from any country for search, rescue and relief. Any relief after was diverted to countries like Indonesia and Sri Lanka, which were more affected. It infact helped Sri Lanka, Maldives and Indonesia in their hour of need. India has now put in place tsunami warning system in Indian Ocean. This will enable administration to get adequate warning to alert the community and facilitate evacuation.

Chapter 11

Global Warming and Related Disasters

What is Global Warming

Rising levels of green house gases together with sulphur dioxide and suspended particulate matters, such as dust etc. in the environment of our living planet i.e. Earth are expected to cause climate change. By absorbing infrared radiation, these gases control the flow of natural energy through the climate system. Among the green house gases, carbon dioxide (CO_2) is currently responsible for over 60 percent of the 'enhanced' Green House Effect, which is responsible for climate change. This gas occurs naturally in the atmosphere but anthropogenic sources and human activities, like deforestation or depletion of land resources are adding much more of this gas (CO_2) into the atmosphere. Current emissions amount to over seven billion tons of carbon, or almost one percent of the total mass of carbon dioxide in the atmosphere. CO_2 produced by human activities, like excessive use of air conditioners, burning forests, smoke stacks pollution emited by vehicles enters the natural carbon cycle. Many billion of tons of carbon are exchanged naturally each year between the atmosphere, the oceans and land vegetation. Global warming is caused by an increase in the temperature of the Earth's lower atmosphere. Global warming is likely to lead to climate changes, resulting from alterations to regional climatic events, such as rainfall patterns, evaporation, rising sea levels etc. Climate induced natural disasters (CINDs) like drought, floods, forest fires and cyclones would become serious problems in coastal areas. Manmade disasters would include ozone depletion, environmental acidification etc.

Due to the concentration of Carbon Dioxide in the atmosphere which presently 380 ppm, the earth has reached a climatic, 'tipping point' since a further increase in carbon dioxide levels will obviously increase the heating of earth which would bring in its wake faster melting of ice caps, rising sea levels, more frequent heat waves, water shortages for upto 250 million people and the risk of extinction for upto 30 percent of all species.

It has been discovered that the protective ozone layer is getting progressively eroded due to impact of increasing human activities (UNEP 1980). The major cause of depletion of ozone layer is the world wide emission of manmade compounds called chlorofloro carbons (CFCs) used in refrigeration, aerosol spray and in many items of daily use. CFCs are by and large chemically inert, having no direct effect on human beings. CFCs which escape into the atmosphere ultimately find their way into the stratosphere where they break down ozone molecules involving complex chemical reactions. Stratospheric ozone is important for the biosphere because it absorbs much of ultra violet (UV) radiation, which is harmful to animals and plants. As increased amount of UV radiation reach the earths surface, human population may be directly affected by increase in skin cancer, eye disorder and suppression of immune system in humans and other living organisms. One percent decline in ozone results in an estimated three percent increase in the potential incidence of skin cancer. In addition, yields of some crops may decline, and irreversible changes may occur in the maritime and other ecosystems, which are exceedingly difficult to predict now.

Inter Govt. Panel in Climate Change (IPCC) of UN in its report has confirmed the global warming trend and has projected that globally average temperature of the air above earth's surface would rise by 1.4 to 5.8°C over the next 100 years. It has already risen by about 1°C since 1900.

India is highly vulnerable to climate change as its economy is heavily dependent on climate sensitive sectors, like agriculture and forestry and its low lying densely populated areas like Orissa, Andhra Pradesh, coastline are threatened by a potential rise in sea level. It appears that progress in climatology and in the development of numerical models, not only enables scientists to relate extreme weather events such as floods and drought, with climate variation, but they can give some insight to climate change scenarios due to global warming, such as sea level rise and changes in frequency, strength and geographical distribution of extreme events. These results should be of great help in taking mitigation measures and formulating correct policies.

Although the science of climate change has been accepted, its politics is still contested with developed nation refusing to take action on reduction of Green House Gases (GHG) unless the developing ones do the same. The developing nations cite their right to develop as an excuse for inaction and put forth their point that developed nations which are the biggest emitters of GHG should curb their emissions first. The climate changes have impacted both developed and developing world. It is interesting to note that these impacts have occurred more in the last decade and have been increasing in frequency and intensity, as predicted by scientists.

Climate Change Induced Disasters

Climate change is likely to have a significant impact on the global environment. The faster the climate change the greater will be the risk of damage. The mean sea level is expected to cause flooding of low lying areas and other damages. Climatic zones including agricultural zones could shift towards the poles. Forests, deserts, rangelands and other unmanaged ecosystems would face new climatic stresses. According to IPCC report, the main threats to the urban population and physical assets of developing cities, affected with more or less intensity based on the actual climate changes, which induce natural disasters, are as follows :

- *A rise in sea level :* 1/3 of global habitation is along coastline. The urban settlements here face the most fundamental challenges from global warming. At risk are also the economic assets in coastal zones. Besides cities and infrastructure, beaches, river floors in estuarine zones and sea erosion are also likely to suffer. Wetlands and tidal flats are subject to flooding. Further more, groundwater risks, increased salinization and coastal acquifers risk diminishing, affecting fresh water supplies and peri-urban agriculture.

- *Tropical Cyclones :* Increasingly frequent and intense tropical and extra-tropical cyclones will cause severe wind damage & storm surges are likely to inundate low-lying coastal regions and cities for longer durations. Ports & other coastal in infrastructure are at risk of damage due to cyclones.
- *Flooding & Landslides :* Expected increase in the scale, intensity and frequency of rainfall in most developing countries will severely strain or overwhelm the storm drainage systems of many urban centres. This could lead to periodic flooding of low lying areas as well as landslides and mudslips on geologically unstable slopes, where informal settlements exist. Cities built next to rivers and on reclaimed lands in river bed planes will be prone to additional inundation.
- *Heat and Cold Waves :* Intense episodes of thermal variability could severly strain urban systems by adding an environmental health risk for more vulnerable segments of the population, imposing extraordinary consumption of energy for heating. This projected change is larger than any climate change experienced over the last 10,000 years.
- *Drought :* Drought though a local phenomenon can be related to large scale or global climate mechanisms. Through the study of atmospheric teleconnection mechanisms between remote areas of the planet, scientists have been able to increasingly link extreme weather events like drought with climate variations and climate change.

Mitigation Policy

Global Level. In 1988, the United Nations Environment Program (UNEP) and the World Meteorological Organisation (WMO) established the Inter Governmental Panel on Climate Change (IPCC), consisting of more than 300 of the World's leading experts to investigate climate change. The IPCC concluded, both in 1990 and in 1992 that a doubling of green houses gases in the atmosphere will lead to serious consequences for the worlds social, economic and natural systems. Among other things, the IPCC concluded that emissions of green house gas from human activities contribute to the natural green house effect and will lead to an additional warming of the atmosphere.

According to UN report, the hole in the ozone layer over Antartica may close within 50 years as the level of destructive ozone depleting CFCs in the atmosphere is declining from a peak of 2.15 parts per million (ppm) in 2000 to 1.15 ppm in 2009. Under the Montreal Protocol the developing countries committed themselves to halving the consumption and production of CFCs by 2005 & to achieving an 85 percent cut by 2007.

Indian Mitigation Policy on Climate Change

Indian Mitigation Policy is based on the following parameters :

- Capacity building at appropriate levels for taking climate change considerations in social, economic & developmental planning.
- Impact assessment including impacts on food and water resources, eco-system and biodiversity, human settlement and human health.
- Promotion of scientific and technological research and systematic observation with a view to further understanding of climate change.
- Education, training and public awareness.
- Enhancement of international cooperation in pursuance of the objectives of the United Nations Framework Convention on Climate Change.

Clean Development Technologies

An attempt is being made all over the world to adopt technologies which would help to reduce energy needs and are non polluting. The focus is presently on following technologies:

- Wind energy
- Solar energy
- Bio diesel
- Hydro power

Environmental scientists have proposed following ten steps to control the global climate change :

- Increasing natural photosynthesis
- Starting natural photosynthesis
- Augmenting $CaCO_3$ sedimentation
- Managing wetlands

- Sequestering water
- Reclaiming deserts
- Limiting animal husbandry
- Burning hydrogenated energies,
- Creating an evolutionary population plan
- Checking deforestation in the short term, enhancing agro forestry and plantations in the medium term and use of advanced technology for efficient forest management in the long term for arresting GHG emissions
- Enhancing the incremental changes in the community participation for arresting climate changes by effective management of land
- Use of GIS technology for mapping agro-ecological zones, vulnerable zones, rain-fed irrigation zones, soil-degradation zones etc. at district level
- Specific case studies on impacts of climate change on ecosystems and water resources in the country should be conducted at micro-level where human dimensions can be incorporated.

Some additional steps which are recommended to be taken immediately are :

- All CFCs must be phased out
- All substitutes should be given rigorous scientific scrutiny for possible contribution to the green house drifts as well as to ozone destruction
- Coal and petroleum to be replaced by natural gas and adding hydrogen to this gas
- Subsidizing the petroleum and nuclear enterprises should be stopped
- Forest destruction must be halted
- Start reforestation through special forces like Ecological Battations consisting of ex-servicemen & others. This experiment has been very successful in Rajasthan, Punjab, U.P., Uttarakhand and Bihar, States of India.
- Survey of mangrove, reef corals and deep-sea corals, for extent, productivity and state of health & possibilities for improvement.

APPENDIX 'E'

How can Community Reduce Carbon Footprints

Travel

1. Use your feet, scooter/motor cycle or mass transportation for most routine transportation needs, whenever possible.
2. If you are in your car, stuck in a traffic jam, try to avoid your car to idle. If you are waiting at a signal or jam for more than 30 seconds, turn off the engine.
3. Purchase radial tyres and keep them adequately inflated to maximise gas mileage.
4. Prefer car pooling to driving alone.
5. Consider flexible work schedules or telecommuting.
6. Car with more than two persons in a car should be allowed to drive in fast lane. Vehicles with single person should move in normal lanes.

Work Place

1. Reduce the need to copy and print. When you have to then use both sides of the paper.
2. Use recycled paper and recycle printer cartridges.
3. Use more reusable water bottles rather than disposable cups.
4. Turn off lights, fans air conditioners, when not in use and at the end of the day. Do not leave it to your peon/helper to do it, at their leisure.
5. If you are using CNG, ensure to fit proper authorised kit.

At Home

- Go easy on air conditioning in summer. At start of summers clean or replace dusty air conditioner filters to keep the air conditioner operating at peak eficiency. Do not keep the air conditioner on for long periods. Switch off air conditioner when room becomes cooler. Switch on fan, it will nearly maintain same temperature, unless you are on the top floor.
- Unplug your electronics when not in use. Turn off the standby mode. To make it easier, use a multiple switchboard or power

strip, as items like your television, computer and cellphone charger still consume power even when turned off.

- Defrost your refrigerator and freezer regularly.
- Replace items only when you really need to. So buy less!!
- Recycle all your paper, glass, aluminium, plastic and electronics too.
- Compost food waste for the garden. Garbage that is not contaminated with degradable (biological) waste can be more easily recycled and sorted, and does not produce methane gas.
- Grow more plants, give them as presents to friends on birthdays/ anniversaries and festival occasions, rather than flower bouquets.
- Encourage energy efficiency at home; switch off lights, fans and ACs and heaters, when leaving the room, even for short duration.
- Switch to compact fluorescent lighting (CFL). CFL bulbs use about 75% less energy than incandescent bulbs and last much longer.
- Use renewable energy like solar and wind, whenever feasible.
- Use cooker for cooking. It consumes much less gas.
- When not in use, switch off the gas cylinder knob to off.
- Conserve Water : Bathe from filled bucket rather than showering. While brushing and shaving, do not keep tap running. Do not wash towels every-day and attend to a leaking tap immediately.

"Somebody asked Jamshedji Tata, "what is one secret of your success, you would like to share with others". He replied, "I switch off the light, when I go out of the room". It conveys a lot of meaning. Keep imagining.

Chapter 12

Chemical and Industrial Disasters

Introduction

Major industrial hazards are generally associated with the potential for fire, explosion or dispersion of toxic chemicals and usually involve release of material from containment followed in the case of volatile materials, by its vaporization & dispersion. Accidents involving major hazards could include:

- Leakage of flammable material, mixing of the material with air, formation of a flammable vapour cloud and drifting of cloud to a source of ignition, leading to a fire or an explosion, affecting the site and possibly populated areas.
- Leakage of toxic material formation of a toxic vapour cloud and drifting of the cloud, affecting directly the site and possibly populated areas.

Leakage of Flammable Material

In the event of release of flammable material, the greatest danger arises from the sudden massive escape of volatile liquids or gases, producing a large cloud of flammable and possibly explosive vapour. If this cloud was ignited, the effect of combustion would depend on many factors, including wind speed and extent to which the cloud was diluted with air. Such hazards can cause a large number of casualties and wholesale damage on site and beyond its boundaries; however the effect is generally limited to a few hundred meters from the site.

Leakage of Toxic Material

Sudden release of large quantities of toxic material has potential to cause deaths and severe injuries at a much greater distance. Actual casualties would depend on population density in the path of cloud and effectiveness of emergency measures like evacuation adopted.

Some chemical and industrial installations pose both types of threats. Moreover, blast and missiles from an explosion can affect the integrity of other plants containing flammable and toxic materials thereby causing an escalation of the disaster, which is also referred to as the 'domino effect'. This happens when due to attraction of power, water and a pool of suitable labour, industry is situated in groups. Such groupings can facilitate the transfer of supplies and products from one site to another.

The release of flammable or toxic materials to atmosphere may therefore lead to an explosion, a fire or the formation of a toxic cloud.

Explosion

Explosions are characterized by a shock wave, which can be heard as a bang and which can cause damage to buildings, breaking windows and ejecting missiles over distances several hundred meters. The injuries and damage are in the first place caused by the shock waves of explosion itself. People are blown over or knocked down and buried under collapsed structures or injured by flying glasses. Although the effect of over pressure can directly result in deaths, this involves only those working in direct vicinity of the explosion.

The effect of the shock waves vary depending on the characteristics of the material, quality involved and the degree of confinement of the vapour cloud. Effects of over pressure are given in Table 12.1.

Table 12.1 : Effects of Explosion over Pressure

Explosion Overpressure	Effect
3.5 kPa (0.5 psi)	> 90% glass breakages > No fatality, very low probability of injury
7 kPa (1 psi)	> Damage to internal partitions and joinery > Injury probability 10%. No. fatality
14 kPa (2 psi)	> House uninhabitable and badly cracked
21 kPa (3 psi)	> Reinforced structures distort > Storage tanks fail > 20% fatality chances to a person in a building
35 kPa (5 psi)	> House uninhabitable > Wagon and plant items over turned. > Threshold of eardrum damage 50% chances of fatality to a person in a building and 15% to a person in open
70 kPa (10 psi)	> Threshold of lung damage > 100% chance of fatality for a person in building or in open

Deflagration and Detonation

Explosions can occur in the form of a deflagration or a detonation depending upon the burning velocity during the explosion. Deflagration occurs when the burning velocity or the flame speed is relatively slow, of the order of 1 m/sec. In a detonation the flame speed is extremely high, 200-300 m/sec. A detonation generates greater pressures and is far more destructive than deflagration. The peak pressure caused by a deflagration to a closed atmospheric vessel reaches 70-80 kPa, whereas a detonation can easily reach a pressure of 200 kPa.

Fig. 12.1 : Explosion in a Factory

Fig. 12.2 : Explosion in a mine

Gas and Dust Explosions

Generally catastrophic gas explosions happen when considerable quantities of flammable material are released and dispersed in air to form an explosive vapour cloud before ignition takes place. Dust explosions occur when flammable solid materials are intensely mixed with air. The dispersed solid material is in the form of powder with very small particle sizes. The explosion occurs following an initiating event such as fire or a small explosion that causes powder that has settled on surfaces to become airborne. Upon mixing with air, the result is secondary explosion which in turn can create a tertiary explosion and so on. Dust explosions have been more common to the agricultural industry. Recently, damaging effects due to dust explosions have been confined to workplace rather than off the plant.

Confined and Unconfined Vapour Cloud Explosions

Confined explosion occur within some sort of containment such as a vessel or pipe work or explosion in a building. Explosions in open air are referred to as unconfined explosions and produce peak pressures of only a few kPa. The peak pressures of confined explosions are generally higher and may reach hundreds of kPa.

Fires

The effects of fire on people take the form of skin burns due to exposure to thermal radiation. The severity of the burns depends on the intensity of the heat and the exposure time. Heat radiation is inversely proportional to the square of the distance from the source. Fires occur in industry more frequently than explosions and toxic release although the consequences in terms of loss of life are generally less. Therefore fires might be considered as having less major hazard potential than explosions and toxic releases. Effects of heat radiation are given in Table 12.2.

Table 12.2 : Effects of Heat Radiation.

Heat Radiation (k W/m^2)	Effect
1.2	Received from sun at noon in summer
2.1	Minimum to cause pain after 1 minute
4.7	Will cause pain in 15-20 seconds and injury after 30 seconds exposure (second degree burns will occur)

contd.....

12.2 table contd.....

12.6	- Significant chance of fatality for extended exposure - Causes temperature of wood to rise to a point where it can be ignited by a naked flame after long exposure - Thin steel with insulation on the side, away from the fire may reach a thermal stress level high enough to cause structural failure.
23	- Likely fatality for extended exposure and chance of fatality for instantaneous exposure. - Spontaneous ignition of wood after long exposure - Unprotected steel will reach thermal stress temperatures which can cause failure - Pressure vessels need to be relieved or failure would occur
35	- Cellulosic material will pilot ignite within one minute's exposure - Significant change of fatality for people exposed instantaneously

Effects of Heat Radiation

Fires can take different forms including jet fire, pool fire, flash fire and boiling liquid expanding vapour explosion (BLEVE). A jet fire would appear as long narrow flame produced eg from an ignited gas pipeline leak. A pool fire would be produced for example, if a release of crude oil from a storage tank into a bund get ignited. A flash fire could occur if an escape of gas reaches a source of ignition and is rapidly burnt back to the source of the release. The BLEVE is generally far more serious than the other fires and cause much more damage in distant places too. This is also discussed in subsequent paras.

Another lethal effect that must be considered in case of fire is the depletion of oxygen in the atmosphere due to consumption of oxygen in the combustion process - generally limited to immediate vicinity. Of importance are also health effects arising from exposure to the fumes generated as a result of fire. These fumes may include toxic gases, such as sulphur dioxide from the combustion of carbon diswphide and nitric oxide from a fire including ammonium nitrate.

Boiling Liquid Expanding Vapour Explosion (BLEVE)

Also referred as a fire ball, a BLEVE is combination of fire and explosion with an intense radiant heat emission within a relatively short time interval. The phenomenon can occur within a vessel or tank in which liquefied gas is kept, above its atmospheric boiling point. If a pressure vessel fails as a result of weakening of its structure, the contents are instantaneously released from the vessel as a turbulent mixture of liquid and gas, expanding rapidly and dispersing in air as a cloud. When this cloud is ignited, a fireball occurs causing an enormous heat radiation intensity within a few seconds. This heat intensity is sufficient to cause severe skin burns and even death at several hundred meters from the vessel. A BLEVE involving a 50 tonne propane tank can cause third degree injuries at distances of approximately 200 meters and blisters at 400 meters. Sometimes it is difficult to make a distinction between a fire and an explosion. Quite often a fire follows an explosion and casualties are caused by both phenomenon.

Toxic Releases

There are large number of chemicals with which particular care needs to be taken to prevent them from having harmful effect on workers. The major discipline of occupational hygiene exist to develop the methods necessary to control exposure to these chemicals possibly over as long a period as the working lifetime of a plant operator. This is of fundamental importance to workers safety. The effects of toxic chemicals when considering major hazards on the other hand are quite different and are concerned with acute exposure during and soon after a major accident rather than with long term chronic exposure. The toxicity of chemicals is commonly determined by using four major methods. These are incident studies, epidemiological studies, animal experiments and micro organism tests. Despite their obvious value these methods suffer from weakness, which means that caution should be exercised in the interpretation of results. Other factors also affect the toxicity of chemicals, for instance age, sex, genetic background, ethnic grouping, nutrition, fatigue, diseases, exposure to other substances with synergistic effects and hours and pattern of work.

Chlorine gas is known to be dangerous to human health at concentration of 10-20 parts per million (ppm) with exposure of 30 minutes. Exposure to chlorine for shorter periods can be fatal at concentration of 100-150 ppm with exposure of even 5-10 minutes. An instantaneous release of 10 tonnes of this chemical may produce a maximum concentration of 140 ppm at a distance of 2 km down wind from the source and of 15 ppm at a distance of 5 km in E weather conditions (stable, normal non-inversion weather). Chlorine and ammonia are toxic chemicals most commonly used in major hazard quantities and both have a history of major accidents. Other chemicals such as methyl isocyanate and dioxin must be used with particular care in view of their higher toxicity, even when used in lesser quantities.

Table 12.3 : Effects of Toxic Gas Emission

Toxic Level	Example
Threshold Limit Value (TLV) is average concentration of the substance in ambient air for a normal 8 hour work day or 40 hours work per week, to which workers may be rapidly exposed, day after day, without a dverse effect	For chlorine it is 1 ppm or 3 mg/m3
Short Term Exposure Limit (STEL) is maximum concentration of substance to which workers may be exposed for a period upto 15 minutes continuously without suffering from irritation, chronic tissue change or narcosis, provided that no more than four excursions per day are permitted, with at least 60 minutes between exposure and that the daily TLV is not exceeded.	3 ppm or a mg/m3
Immediate Danger to Life and Health (IDLH) is maximum concentration of the substance to which a healthy male worker can be exposed for a short time with immediate danger to life or irreversible organ system damage.	25 ppm or 75 mg/m3

Transportation of Hazardous Goods

We have witnessed rapid growth in transportation of hazardous chemicals by road. Major road accidents have clearly demonstrated that hazardous chemical carriers, when involved in accident, can cause disastrous consequences like fire, explosion and spillage, resulting in loss of life and property, besides environmental pollution. Such accidents demand immediate availability of essential information to take appropriate counter measures.

The products of chemical industry vary enormously in their types, property and degree of hazard, ranging from explosive to plaster board. These are transported as solids, liquids or gases in a wide range of temperatures and pressures. Under the new MV Act, every motor vehicle carrying hazardous substance should comply with certain regulations, important among them are :

- The vehicle should have emergency information panels on both sides and in the rear. In addition, relevant UN Hazard class label (UN symbol) has to be displayed on the front part of the vehicle. (Central Motor Vehicles Rules 129 to 137).
- The driver of vehicle should possess the 'Transport Emergency Card' or Trem Card (Central Motor Vehicles Rule 132 (3) Annexure V).
- The driver of vehicle should be able to read and write at least one Indian language out of those specified in the VII Schedule of the Constitution and English (Amendment in 1993).

Emergency Information Panel : It provides information in case of an emergency. It indicates the correct technical name of the substance being transported, its UN Number, hazchem code and UN hazard class label. The panel also provides a contact number in an emergency as also specialist advice. Each term in the Emergency Panel is explained below :

UN Number : The UN Committee has classified various hazard substances according to the risk involved. Each hazardous substance included in the list has been allocated a four digit number which is substances "UN number". So far there are over three thousand chemicals which have been allotted numbers. As numbers are in Arabic letters, it helps ready identification of the chemical being transported.

Hazchem Code : The Hazchem code is an emergency code designed by the London Fire Brigade. It enables the fire brigade for the actions to be taken in case of fire, spillage or leakage. It also ensures the use of appropriate protective clothing if any evacuation is required. The Hazchem code consists of numbered or one or two letters which indicate the required actions.

Class label : Chemicals have been grouped into nine basic classes based on the nature of hazard, represented numerically from 1 to 9. Many of these classes are further separated with divisions. They are :

Class 1 : Explosives

Class 2 : Gases-compressed, liquified, dissolved under pressure or deeply refrigerated.

Class 3 : Flammable liquids.

Class 4	:	Flammable solids substances liable to spontaneous combustion, substances which on contact with water emit flammable gases.
Class 4.1	:	Flammable Solids.
Class 4.2	:	Substances liable to spontaneous combustion.
Class 4.3	:	Substances which when in contact with water emit flammable gases.
Class 5	:	Oxidizing substances, organic peroxides.
Class 5.1	:	Oxidizing substances.
Class 5.2	:	Organic peroxides.
Class 6	:	Poisonous (toxic) substances.
Class 6.1	:	Infectious substances.
Class 7	:	Radio active substances.
Class 8	:	Corrosives.
Class 9	:	Miscellaneous dangerous substances.

Each United Nations Hazard Class label (with the exception of class 9) has a distinctive diamond shaped label bearing as pictogram for quick hazard recognition. Each label also has a characteristic background colour.

Hazard Type	**Colour**
Explosives	Orange
Flammable	Red
Water reactive	Blue
Oxidizing Substances	Yellow
Toxic/Infections	White
Radio active	Yellow & White
Corrosive	Black & White

The advantage of this system is that the shape, colour and pictogram of the label clearly convey the nature of dangers in the chemicals being transported. It also helps overcome language barriers and literacy problems; extremely beneficial in a multi-lingual country like India. Besides, dangerous goods in transit are recognized from a distance. The danger of the risk is made more apparent by means of black symbol each representing a particular risk. For example, if the flame denoting risk of fire, the upper half of the diamond shaped label (square set at an angle of 45°) is reserved for the black symbol representing the nature of the risk. The reference symbols are provided for each UN Class. The number of the class or division is shown in black colour in the bottom corner of the label.

Term Card

Under the Act, every vehicle of dangerous goods has to carry a Transport Emergency Card. The Emergency Information Panel only provides very essential data to enable immediate actions to be taken in case of a mishap. However, detailed instructions on fire, spillage or leakage and action to deal with the emergency are indicated in the Trem card. The card is to be provided by the consignor and is to be carried by the driver in his cabin. This will help the driver to act responsibly because he has been given information in writing on the immediate action that should be taken in the event of an emergency.

Mitigation measures for Chemical and Industrial accidents are given in Appendix 'F' (Page 201).

How to handle various types of chemical disasters are given at Appendix 'G' (Page 204).

annexure contd...

APPENDIX 'F'

CHEMICAL AND INDUSTRIAL DISASTER MITIGATION

There are two main stakeholders in prevention of industrial and chemical accidents. The district authorities and the industry. Both have their distinct roles and responsibilities to play in mitigating chemical and industrial disasters. At the national level, Ministry of Environment and Forest is the nodal Ministry for Chemical and Industrial Disasters.

District Authorities

The public authorities should set general safety objectives, establish a clear and coherent control framework and ensure, through appropriate enforcement measures that all relevant requirements are being met. The authorities should set systems for :

- The identification and notification of hazardous installations.
- Monitoring of such installations.
- Developing new approaches for accident prevention, identifying the tools needed.
- Ensuring that there is adequate reporting, response mechanism and post mortem (investigation) of accidents.
- Coordination mechanism between all stake holders, viz relevant public authority, industry, corporate associations (like FICCI, CII) independent experts, trade unions, interest groups and the public.
- Enforcement mechanism should include suitable sanctions, with penalties for non compliance of any requirement.

Accident Prevention

For effective accident prevention, safety considerations should be incorporated among other things :

- Planning and construction of installations.
- Operating policies & procedures, including organization and personnel arrangements.
- Monitoring and assessment of safety
- Operation shutdown.

Other Measures

- Promotion of training programs.
- Encouragement of research.
- Fostering public awareness.

Industry

The management of the Industries should formulate a safety policy. Safety should be an integral part of business activities of the enterprise. Aim should be to reach the ultimate goal of ' zero incidents' and resources and capacity building should be targeted towards this goal. Progress towards this goal can be achieved by :

- Establishing safety related objectives.
- Disclose these objectives to workers.
- Measuring progress towards achievement of the objectives.
- Learn lessons from incidents already happened.
- As part of the safety culture, there should be commitment.
- Surprise checks to confirm adherence to safety norms.
- Conduct table top and mock exercises periodically to validate the safety norms and DM Plans.

The management has the following responsibility during the various phases of disaster.

Planning and Construction

- Hazard identification and assessment.
- Engineering design as per building code.
- Construction by trained masons as per design of qualified architects and structural engineers.
- Transfer of technology to other stakeholders.
- Acquisitions and affiliated operations.

Operations

- Safety procedures and arrangements.
- Organisation and personnel and role & responsibilities of each.
- Education and training of workers and management at various lands.

- Human factors.
- Maintenance of strict compliance monitoring.
- Repairs and modifications to be carried out immediately.
- Storage of hazardous substances, special considerations to be taken into account.

Safety Performance Review and Evaluation

- Safety performance review.
- Monitoring by industry experts.
- Monitoring by district administration and inspector of factories.

Emergency Preparedness and Response

The management should formulate an 'on site' plan by Disaster Management experts. 'On site' plan should have complete range of credible accident scenarios. Plan should nominate a site incident controller and site main controller operating from the emergency control room. The response mechanism should be earmarked and should be ready to be operational in the quickest time frame. Table top and mock exercises should be conducted periodically with all seriousness of a professional. The response team should be carefully selected and trained. Adequate medical facilities should be made available. The 'on site' plans should be reviewed by management with help from disaster management experts, atleast once in a year, after a mock exercises.

"Off Site" Emergency Preparedness Plan

It should be made by the district administration with inputs from the industry. The plan should have an objective, provide relevant information on the hazardous installations and surrounding areas, evaluate the hazards which may result in emergency situations for the community and establish procedures to be followed and officials responsible in the event of an accident/disaster.

All stake holders like police, fire and emergency services, civil defence, public works and utilities, management of the industrial units, health and environmental agencies etc. should be in know of the "off site" plan, which should be practised at least once a year, in consultation with and under the umbrella of the district administration.

APPENDIX 'G'

EMERGENCY PROCEDURE FOR HANDLING CHEMICAL DISASTERS

Hazcam Tanker / Truck Accident

- If possible, drive out of populated areas and switch off the engine.
- Identify the cargo, refer to labels and Trem Card Instructions.
- In case of a major leak or highly inflammable gas/vapour, do not start the engine. If it is a small leak, see if it can be arrested easily.
- Request on-lookers to leave the affected area.
- Stop pilferage of the leaked substance. It can be dangerous.
- Secure/isolate the accident area & divert traffic.
- Remove affected persons for first aid.
- In the event of electrical fire, isolate the battery of the vehicle.
- In case of fire, inform nearest fire station, avoid inhalation of fumes, use gas masks, if required.
- Contain small spill by covering it with sand.
- Avoid direct contact with skin. Wear necessary protective clothing like PVC apron.
- In case of contact with eye or skin, wash with plenty of water. For any major contamination, remoe clothing immediately and take bath.

How to Handle Chemicals

- Be serious! and be careful while handling chemicals at all times.
- Treat all chemicals with respect. They should be handled carefully.
- Do not take shortcuts and do not be too over confident.
- Follow your supervisor's directions and wear protective clothing and equipment when needed.
- In areas where chemicals are being handled, stored or used, there should be no smoking, no drinking and no eating.
- Read and follow the warning sign in your work area. Read the labels on all containers before you move them, before you open them and before you use the contents.

- Keep yourself and your work area clean.
- Objects lying on ground can be hazardous and even small spills can be slippery.
- Wash your hands thoroughly with soap and water after handling any chemical. Always wash up before eating, smoking or using toilet facilities.
- Before unloading chemicals from freight cars or trucks, check the containers to see if any are cracked, broken or leaking. If they are, report to your supervisor.
- When there is a spill or leak, extinguish all sources of flame or sparks, shut off the leak, if safe to do so. Inform your supervisor for further instructions. If spillage is not checked, evacuate area immediately and re-enter only when you are wearing the protective equipment.
- Never flush chemicals in a public sewer or allow vapours. Some chemicals can be hazardous in concentration and to low to detect by smell.
- In a plant, ventilation is first line of defence. When ventilation is not adequate and concentration of a chemical in the air is above the safe limits, wear a respirator. Check its operation before use. If respirator fails, leave the area and remove the mask immediately.

Fire and Fire Hazards

- Chemical fires can start easily and spread quickly.
- Remove the source of fire or sparks from the areas where chemicals are stored or used. No smoking, no welding, no burning and no machinery or electrical equipment that produces sparks should be allowed.

Flammable Chemicals

- These chemicals catch fire easily at normal temperature and vapours can explode from a spark, flame or heat source.
- The vapour of nearly all flammable chemicals are heavier than air and hence they can 'crawl' along the ground to distant flames and sparks, then flash back to source.
- Keep all containers of flammable liquids closed when not in use. After use, re-close the container tightly.

- Empty containers are dangerous. They may contain harmful chemical vapours or liquid residues.
- If a fire starts :
  - Ring the alarm quickly
  - Rescue injured people
  - If fire is small, try to put it off if you can do it safely. However, personal safety is important.
  - Do not try to put out large fires without assistance. Leave it to Fire Services. Evacuate the area.
  - Minimize your exposure to fumes and vapours from a fire. Many chemicals give off poisonous gases when they burn, wear respirator when in chemical fire area.
  - If fire is near tanks and drums of flammable chemicals, heat from nearby fire may cause them to explode. Spray water on these containers to keep them cool.

Swallowing

- If someone has swallowed a chemical : In some cases, induced vomiting is not advisable as they can be more dangerous than swallowing.
- For induced vomiting, have the victim stick his finger down his throat until he vomits. If this does not work, give him several glasses of milk or water and try again. After vomiting, give him another glass of milk or water and take him to a doctor. Never give anything by mouth to an unconscious person.

Inhalation

If a fellow worker is overcome by gases or vapours, remove victim to fresh air and call for medical help. Remove any object that is in his mouth and keep him warm. If person is not breathing, do not wait. Give artificial respiration right away. Continue until victim can breathe on his own or until medical help arrives.

Fire Extinguishers

- use of wrong type of fire extinguisher can be dangerous. Example using water on some solvents can spread fire.

- Use state of the art 'mist technology' fire extinguishers which can be used for all types of fires. Such back pack extinguishers are also light and can do the same work as 4000-5000 litre water tankers.

First Aid

- Learn first aid procedures.
- *Minimize your contact with all chemicals :* Some chemicals can cause rashes, other actually burn your skin. Some can penetrate through your skin and make you feel sick and even damage internal organs.
- *While handling chemicals* if you experience eye discomfort, breathing difficulty, dizziness, headache, nausea, vomiting or skin irritation, stop whatever you are doing, leave the area and obtain first aid if necessary.
- *Burns :* Keep victim calm and cover him with blanket to keep him warm but not hot. Get medication as early as possible.
- *Eye contact :* Flush your eyes for 15 minutes with large amount of water. Use the nearest tap or fountain or any source of clean water. Make sure to keep your eyes, wide open while splashing water.
- *Skin Contact :* Wash with lots of soap and water and disinfectant with waterless hand cleaner, if needed. If chemical is still on skin, use small amount of solvent like Acetone for washing. Do not use solvent for clean up. They remove natural oil from skin.
- *Leather goods* (belt, shoes etc.) are difficult to clean and you may have to destroy them if they cannot be decontaminated.

case study contd...

Case Study

Bhopal Gas Tragedy 1984

Introduction

The Bhopal gas tragedy was a catastrophe that has no parallel in industrial disasters in the world. Pollution is caused primarily by the affluent. The effects of the pollution are mostly felt by the poor victims in the developing and underdeveloped countries. While as development is essential to improve the quality of life, it is equally essential to ensure that development takes place on a sustainable basis. There are many instances of environmental disruptions due to poorly conceived plans. The major offenders are petroleum, steel, organic chemicals and paper industries. Bhopal Gas Tragedy falls under the organic chemical industrial disasters. The chemical process industry (CPI); the business market related to the Bhopal disaster is the type of industry responsible for synthesizing base chemicals for components in commercial products.

Background

Union Carbide's operations in India go back to 1924, when the Union Carbide Corporations (UCC), a US based company opened an assembly plant for batteries in Calcutta. In 1983, Union Carbide had 14 plants in India producing chemical pesticides, batteries and other products. UCC operations in India were conducted through Union Carbide India Limited (UCIL). UCC held 50.9% of UCIL stock and remaining 49.1% was owned by various Indian investors. At that time maximum ownership for a foreign investor was only 40%, but it was waived off in case of Union Carbide by the Government of India because of the sophistication of its technology and company's potential for export.

The Bhopal plant was licensed to manufacture 5250 tons of Methyl Isocyanate (MIC) based pesticides per year. However, peak production was only 2704 tons in 1981, falling to 1657 tons in 1983. Thus quantity of pesticide manufactured in 1983 was only 31.37 % of its licensed capacity. Was Bhopal plant used for experiments in processes for which UCIL was not authorised? Or was the capacity of the plant under utilized to maintain monopolistic hold over prices. The losses of the Company in 1984 itself amounted to more than Rs. 45 crores. Ultimately, UCC decided to close the plant and dismantle, and take it to a South American country.

Early Warning

In October 1982, a mixture of MIC chloroform and hydrochloric acid escaped from the Bhopal plant, endangering the neighbouring community and injuring a few workers. This was a warning which made it clear of potential public risks but due to Carbide officials insistence for following strict safety precautions there was no action taken. All this, coupled with a series of accidents that occured in the plant and the gloomier prospects for its turnaround, served as a signal for many well trained and experienced engineers and operators to leave Bhopal plant for more greener pastures elsewhere, outside India. Between half to 2/3 No of engineers who were familiar with the plant right from the project stage had left Bhopal factory before the accident.

What Happened and Why?

MIC in gaseous form is heavier than air and has a tendency to settle down. In this form it is subject to wind dispersal. The geographical characteristics of the area would control the dispersal. At about 11:00 PM on December 02, 1984 the pressure in tank No. 610 started building up. 41 tons of MIC gas in this tank, burst from a gas scrubber and leaked into atmosphere between 12:45 AM to 1:30 AM on 03 December 1984. The cloud of gas dispersed across the plant grounds and in the morning the toxic bog enveloped most of the area in and around Bhopal. No alarm ever sounded a warning and no evacuation plan was existing or executed. It was only when the sun rose on 3 December 1984 that the magnitude of the devastation became clear. Although there was no casuality within the Union Carbide premises, dead bodies of humans and animals blocked the strcets, leaves turned black and there was smell of burning chilli pepper lingering in the air. Although official figure of death is about 3000, more than 10,000 people are reported to have died unoffically and more than 600,000 were affacted. 30,000 to 50,000 were too ill to ever return to their jobs. This was indeed the Hiroshima of Chemical Industry. Legal battle ensued for compensation which got finally settled by Supreme Court of India ordering Union Carbide to pay up US $ 470 million, which worked out to mere Rs. 10,000 per victim. The estimatd victims were calculated to be 3000 at the time of out of court settlement of compensation between UCC and Govt. of India and hence the compensation amount for each victim got drastically reduced. This was the civil case. In the criminal case, the head of UCC Mr. Anderson was allowed to go back to USA and only 8 Indian management personnel of UCIL have been finally convicted after 26 years and given two years imprisonment, by a lower court, which is considered highly inadequate.

Scene Inside Union Carbide Factory on 03 December 1984.

Lessons Learnt

The following broad lessons can be learnt from the disaster:

- The tragedy was caused by synergy of the very worst of American and Indian cultures. An American Corporation cynically used a third world country to escape from increasing strict safety standards imposed at home, for handling hazardous materials.

- Fall in safety standards.
- Gradual but sustained erosion of good practices in the plant.
- Declining quality of technical training of plant personnel especially in supervisory staff.
- Depleting inventory of vital spares.
- An indiscriminate economy drive that starved the plant of necessary capital replacement and created general demoralisation in the staff.
- Exodus of some of the more experienced and able engineers and operators from the factory, due to its impending closure.
- Increasing under manning of important work stations in many parts of the plant.
- There was an 'on site' Emergency Plan which saved the lives of personnel in the plant but 'off site' Emergency Plan was not made. The general public was not aware of what to do in case of an emergency. When all they were required to do was to put a wet cloth on their faces and breathe through it. Water mostly absorbs toxic effects. The district administration alongwith Union Carbide management are to be blamed for not having an effective and periodically practised 'off site' plan. All hazardous industries must have 'off site' plan and it must be practised regularly, atleast once a year. The plan should be updated after 'off-site' mock drill if required.
- The hazardous industry was located in a populated area. The busy railway station was very near, which affected passengers when trains halted as per normal halt.
- The State Government gave the industrial unit a clean chit even when in 1982, a gas leak took place, speaks of the ignorance or corruption in Indian polity.
- The legal system failed the victims and then began to consider reforms. The legal regime requires radical reorientation.
- Given the open new economic policy, a number of multinationals are coming/likely to invest in every conceivable sector in India, due to cheap labour and big market. The laws should make them accountable and victims able to sue these companies in their

country of origin or the companies be made liable to jurisdiction of Indian Courts.

- Those who survived MIC leaks, the nightmare is a lingering one. They still suffer from extensive lung damage, birth of deformed children and no adequate health care for the victims, although a decent hospital was constructed by UCIL for victims of the Bhopal gas tragedy.
- Environmental Impact Assessment (EIA) has been made mandatory for hazardous industries. It is a preventive process which avoids costly mistakes in planning and development. EIA should be carried out during feasibility study stage itself.
- Bhopal Gas Tragedy became a boon for other areas, like in Delhi, all hazarous industries were shifted out of the city. The Ministry of Environment and Forest, reviewed the existing laws. The loopholes were identified, new manuals and safety norms were formulated and views of the stakeholders were taken. The Environment (Protection) Act 1986, The Factories Act 1948, as amended in 1976 and 1987 and The Natural Environment Tribunal Act 1995, came into being after the Bhopal Gas Tragedy. There was a relook again and the gaps in safety were further cemented by making 'on site' and 'off site' mandatory for hazardous and polluting industries, by DM Act, 2005 and Guidelines on Chemical (Inducted) Disasters issued by NDMA.